AA PO KU-412-494

ORLANDO

Written by Lindsay Hunt
Peace and Quiet section
by Paul Sterry

© Automobile Association
Developments Limited 1993, 2002.
First published 1993 as *Essential
Orlando and Walt Disney World*
Revised second edition 1995
Reprinted November 1996
Reprinted as *Pocket Guide Orlando
and Walt Disney World* 2000
Reprinted 2002, 2003

Maps © Automobile Association
Developments Limited 1993, 2002.

Published and distributed in the
United Kingdom by AA Publishing, a
trading name of Automobile
Association Developments Limited,
whose registered office is
Millstream, Maidenhead Road,
Windsor, Berkshire SL4 5GD.
Registered number 1878835.

A CIP catalogue record for this book
is available from the British Library.

ISBN 0 7495 2476 6

Automobile Association
Developments Limited retains the
copyright in the original edition
© 1993 and in all subsequent
editions, reprints and amendments.

All rights reserved. No part of this
publication may be reproduced, stored
in a retrieval system, or transmitted in
any form or by any means – electronic,
photocopying, recording or otherwise
– unless the written permission of the
publishers has been obtained
beforehand. This book may not be
sold, resold, hired out or otherwise
disposed of by way of trade in any
form of binding or cover other than that
in which it is published, without the
prior consent of the publisher.
The contents of this publication are
believed correct at the time of printing.
Nevertheless, the publishers cannot be
held responsible for any errors or
omissions or for changes in the details
given in this guide or for the
consequences of any reliance on the
information provided by the same. This
does not affect your statutory rights.
Assessments of attractions, hotels,
restaurants and so forth are based
upon the author's own experience and,
therefore, descriptions given in this
guide necessarily contain an element
of subjective opinion which may not
reflect the publisher's opinion or
dictate a reader's own experience on
another occasion.
**We have tried to ensure accuracy in
this guide, but things do change and
we would be grateful if readers
would advise us of any inaccuracies
they may encounter.**

A01577

Colour separation by: BTB Colour
Reproduction Ltd, Whitchurch,
Hampshire

Printed by: Printers Trento S.R.L.,
Italy

Front cover picture: *Parade
through Main Street USA,
Walt Disney World.*

Maps and Plans

Contents

This book employs a
simple rating system to
help choose which places
to visit:

✓	'top ten' theme parks

 ◆◆◆ do not miss
 ◆◆ see if you can
 ◆ worth seeing if you
have time

Introduction and Background

INTRODUCTION

The Florida package suggests glamourous beach-life, national parks, fragile ecosystems, and flourishing orange groves. Not much of this applies to Orlando. Sunshine? Mmm, a bit sultry. Cool it with a coastal breeze on that soft white sand around the Keys. Scenery, then? Central Florida's countryside is fairly uninteresting – flat, lots of unsightly urban sprawl, trailer homes, scrubby pines and withered orange trees. Head south for the Everglades if you are interested in natural habitats. Peace and quiet, a get-away-from-it-all holiday? Absolutely not – are you crazy? So what is all the hype about this strange boom town in the middle of failed citrus groves? Answer, theme parks. This is definitely the main reason for visiting Orlando on holiday. Not sure you are so keen on theme parks? Then consider this. If you have never seen Orlando, you have never seen theme parks. These are the biggest, brightest, brassiest of their kind, anywhere in the world. They are on a scale you cannot imagine.

Biggest of all is the Walt Disney World resort, almost as big as San Francisco (twice the size of Manhattan), and still growing with mesmerising speed, engulfing the whole region like some giant bubble. If it ever bursts, the effects will be shattering for the local economy. Walt Disney World is not *all* of Orlando by any means, but it is definitely the focal point. You cannot possibly visit this part of the USA and not see WDW.

There are those who gnash their teeth over Disney and his fellow theme-parkers, accusing them of reducing the universe to 'a sickening blend of cheap formulas packaged to sell', where life is mediocre, blandly safe, and trivially happy. Walt Disney World appeals to children of all ages, but it is Peter Pan land. Here fairy tales are stripped of Grimmer aspects or nasty Freudian connotations, while mermaids are decently covered up with bra-tops.

If today's mass culture of television and computerised technology appalls you, if you prefer to nourish your children on a diet of improving books, Orlando may not be for you. But only the most puritanical believe an occasional hamburger will ruin your life for ever. And that is what Orlando is like – an enormous plateful of the most calorific, imaginative, appetising junk food you will ever taste.

High-quality junk too, however much a contradiction in terms that sounds. Orlando's theme parks, strongly influenced by Walt Disney World, have their own brand of classiness. It exists in their cleanliness, their spick-and-span tidiness, the rigorous standards of maintenance everywhere. Anyone used to less efficient regimes will marvel at the speed and skill with which such vast numbers of people can be moved about, as well as at the courteous and considerate way in which it is done. You will have to queue in Orlando's theme parks (a lot!), but you will not feel

Mickey Mouse

Imaginative design at Orlando extends to the skyline

herded, as tourists so often are. Those cheerful, ever-smiling staff (the 'cast', in Disney parlance) know how to make you, the guest, top dog (visitors are always called 'guests' at WDW, never 'customers'). Litter, disorder, negligence, surliness – these deficiencies are not part of Orlando's world. It is salutary to experience this once in a while, and discover just how well things can be done.

Walt Disney was responsible for these unprecedented standards of Orlando hospitality, posthumously importing his well-tried theme park formula from that other Orange County in California. Outside Walt Disney World there may be people who do *not* wish you a nice day – indeed, a few who plainly could not care less whether you have one or not. Some visitors prefer this closer approximation to the real world to the never-never land of The Magic Kingdom. But the contrast may make you realise, and appreciate, just how much effort those Disney folk put into smiling at you.

Would *you* enjoy Orlando? There is no absolute guarantee, but if you ask the millions who flood through those turnstiles each year if they did enjoy it, most of them say yes, sometimes rather to their surprise.

BACKGROUND

For many visitors, Orlando means Walt Disney World. Hardly surprising, since WDW is the most popular man-made tourist destination on earth. It is now more than 20 years since the Mouse arrived in Florida from his first theme park home in Disneyland, California. Things have changed so rapidly in the area since then that few can remember what life was like in those olden days. Disney was by no means the first theme-parker in Orlando. There were a number of attractions all doing just fine before Walt Disney World swung Florida's centre of gravity firmly inland from the coastal regions. One of Disney's most significant rivals in Orlando today is Anheuser–Busch, the brewers of Budweiser and Michelob, who own three major attractions in the area (Sea World, Cypress Gardens and Busch Gardens). The arrival of Universal Studios from Hollywood and its development into Universal Orlando has has also put Walt Disney World on its mettle. But few would deny Disney's pre-eminence in Orlando.

In 1970, the year before WDW opened, only five per cent of Florida's tourists bothered to visit the central plains. Today it is something over a third. Some of the older attractions, such as the Cypress Gardens, are still going strong, albeit with drastic improvements and renovations. Others, like Boardwalk and Baseball, have succumbed to competition, caught in the slipstream of Disney's unstoppable juggernaut. The lakes and springs north and west of Orlando provide popular recreational lungs for outdoor types. Florida's coastal magnets still draw hordes, but overdevelopment and the rising crime rate have done much to dent the former popularity of the Gold Coast. Although some parts of Miami are very attractive, other areas are dangerous, and some of the coastal developments are very ugly.

So what is it like, this central belt of the Sunshine State? Scenically, no great shakes. It is very flat, with stands of slash pines and scrubland marking uncultivated ground, though just north of the Orlando area you will

*Disney's Big
Thunder Mountain*

Hollywood, WDW

find the central highlands, part of the Ocala rock ridge. Lakes, rivers and springs indicate how surprisingly waterlogged this hot region is: the mosquito-infested swamps where alligators skulk in the reedbeds have not yet all been drained. Before the theme park era, when cattle-ranching was one of Florida's economic mainstays, alligators were a serious hazard to young or sick livestock. The cowhands (locally known as 'crackers') learned, the hard way, how to deal with these dim-witted but dangerous reptiles. Alligators are now a lucrative source of income, and are farmed for their attractively mottled skins. Ironically, it is sometimes the former crackers who tend them, wrestling with their vice-like jaws in muddy ditches to entertain passing tourists.

Florida's other economic miracle, of course, is oranges. A vast proportion of the world's concentrated citrus juice is produced here, though most of the successful farms lie south of Orlando, where blight and frost have wreaked havoc among the local groves. Walt Disney's father once had an unsuccessful shot at growing oranges in Florida. Perhaps Walt's decision to buy up that huge chunk of central Florida and turn it into gold was some subconscious filial vengeance on the land that refused to grant his father a decent living. Wherever you drive around Orlando, you will see the sad, withered skeletons of orange trees killed in the last big freeze. Some farmers have doggedly replanted; others have turned to less sensitive plants like strawberries and sweetcorn, or to tourism. But Walt Disney World's address is Orange County, Florida, and evermore shall be so.

Orlando, the seat of Orange County, covers a vast, sprawling metropolitan area across three counties, and is still rapidly expanding, with immigration currently running at just over 1,000 new residents a week. About a quarter of its inhabitants make a living from tourism. Its permanent population is about a million, but it is annually inundated by over 13 million tourists, who obviously contribute vast profits (something like $5 billion in 1992) to its coffers, and in return place huge strains on its

Re-creating the American dream

resources. The potential for ecological damage caused by Orlando's booming tourism industry is only just dawning, and scientists are casting very anxious eyes on the Everglades National Park, where most of Orlando's industrial and domestic pollution eventually winds up. Walt Disney's touching faith in technological progress as a universally Good Thing would take a few knocks were he still alive today. Before Disney, the Orlando area had around 6,000 hotel rooms. Now it has something like 80,000 (which is more than New York!), with more to come. Disney owns and operates about 12 per cent of these. The Walt Disney World resort has about 33,000 permanent staff, and is by far the biggest employer in central Florida. After US visitors, the largest group of tourists in recent years has come from Britain, followed by rapidly increasing numbers from Latin America.

Besides Walt Disney World, the Orlando area has received much publicity and a considerable amount of associated industrial development from its proximity to Cape Canaveral, launch-pad of the US space programme since the 1960s.

Orlando now hosts an enormous slice of the USA's lucrative convention (conference) market (many of its hotels are specifically geared for that), and many large companies have moved their head offices here. In comparison with other parts of Florida, particularly Miami, its population is young and sprightly, fully able to take advantage of the area's remarkable range of sports and outdoor amenities.

Orlando is an undistinguished place, though not unpleasant or dangerous compared with some large American cities. A few bits of older architecture have been saved (or more accurately, carefully reproduced) to amuse tourists, but these scarcely form integral parts of the modern city, and now seem as artificial as its theme park attractions. There is little reason to venture downtown and explore, still less to stay in the city centre; the most you are likely to see is a few high-rises as you bypass the city on Interstate Highway 4, or the areas that you pass through on the way to its few central sights, such as Church Street Station. Most of the metropolitan area merges into an ugly mishmash of billboards, shopping malls, motels and gas stations, with multi-lane highways stretching in all directions. An exception is the pleasant northerly residential district of Winter Park, perhaps the only place in Orlando you might go to for its intrinsic appeal.

Historically, Orlando's pedigree amounts to little more than an encampment for soldiers fighting the Seminole Indian War at the beginning of the 19th century. The name is alleged to refer to one Orlando Reeves, a scout who spied a log rolling suspiciously towards him one night while on watch, fired at it, and thus saved his fellow campers from an untimely ambush by Indians. The unfortunate Orlando, however, was killed by the arrow the 'log' had already launched at him. The city was officially given its present name in 1857.

Most of Orlando's attractions lie southwest of the city, easily reached via Interstate Highway 4, the most useful road artery in the area. All the life-support systems tourists need are within this area, and the Walt Disney World resort is completely self-contained, like a space station on some distant planet. It barely seems to interact with its neighbourhood at all – a deliberate policy. Walt Disney did his best to keep the outside world and its undesirable influences at bay, not wishing to make the same mistake he had with Disneyland in California, now besieged by hideous urban sprawl. Walt wanted his new Magic Kingdom to sustain the illusions he conjured into it. Once within Walt Disney World's Maingate, you enter another world. When you leave its confines, you may well see Walt's point.

Just one of many pavilions at EPCOT

EPCOT's Spaceship Earth and the monorail

Walt Disney – The Dreamfinder

In EPCOT Center you will find *Journey into Imagination*. It is not one of WDW's best efforts, but its theme would probably have appealed a lot to Walt. Based on the film *Honey, I Shrunk the Kids*, in it you will witness a quest for new ideas, eternally optimistic about future progress. Not unlike Disney himself.

Successful tycoons come and go, but few have captured so many imaginations, influenced so many people, aroused such controversy, such passionate loyalties and loathings, and such enormous interest, as Walt Disney. Journalists devote years to analysing his life and work; articles and books proliferate on the subject of his empire, weighing its benign or malignant influences. Walt Disney has been dead for over 30 years, yet through the huge and vastly powerful organisation he set in motion he has achieved an alarming degree of immortality. Mickey Mouse, his most memorable creation, is now over 65 years old, but in his bright new coating he looks set to outlive any number of ephemeral Turtles or Muppets. In a survey asking people to name the top ten Americans most successful in business, Walt Disney came second only to Henry Ford, and way ahead of those awesome heroes Carnegie and Rockefeller.

Walter Elias Disney came from humble origins, his father a struggling Mid-Westerner whose varied enterprises consistently failed. When they did, he upped sticks and moved his wife and their five children to pastures new. Walt had a scrappy education, and spent his spare time living on his wits, selling newspapers on street corners, hawking sodas on trains, painting camouflage helmets, and discovering a marked if not outstanding talent for drawing. The family had moved to Kansas City, and it was here, in 1920, that Walt decided to try his hand at cartoon shorts and advertisements. Within three years he was bankrupt. Walt, undaunted, went to Hollywood and, after many false starts and financial failures, achieved some sort of a living in animated silent cartoons, in partnership with his elder brother Roy.

Old Peking under Orlando skies

BACKGROUND

The backlot,
Universal Studios

Losing control of his most successful cartoon character, Oswald the Rabbit, to an unprincipled New York distributor taught Walt a lesson he never forgot about trusting people. Walt, thoroughly down on his luck and wiped out of cash, began idly doodling on the long train journey from New York back to Hollywood – or so the story goes. The rough outline took shape somewhere in Ohio or Kansas. It was a mouse.

Mickey's success developed gradually over many years. He acquired a circle of friends – Donald Duck, Goofy, Pluto – and enabled the Disney brothers to set up a new studio, Walt Disney Productions.

Roy Disney tried to temper Walt's wilder impulses with notes of sensible financial caution, but Walt, always cavalier about the money side of things, was the enthusiast, the ideas man, a huge risk-taker, a born entrepreneur. If he did not have the necessary artistic gifts to make the most of the exciting new cinematic technology, he knew a man who did, and slowly the Disney empire began to prosper, with blockbusting, full-length feature animations like *Snow White*, *Pinocchio* and *Fantasia*.

From full-length animations Walt tried his hand at live-action historical adventure films, comedies and wildlife pictures. *Davy Crockett* and *Mary Poppins* contributed vastly to the Disney coffers. The core of the business was always good, clean, family entertainment for those post-war baby boomers. With enormous prescience, the Disneys seized the opportunities presented by the new era of television, while fellow cinema moguls crumbled before the small screen.

Above all, Walt was a weaver of stories (and a shameless borrower of them), by all accounts a gifted raconteur and a brilliant editor. All his life he worked absurdly, obsessively hard, even coming dangerously close to a nervous breakdown in 1931. When they arrived in the mornings his staff would find little notes on blue paper waiting to inform them about wilted flowers or burned-out light bulbs, the result of Walt's nocturnal wanderings to exercise his passion for order and neatness. He led an exemplary settled and happy domestic life with his wife and two daughters – and a miniature steam train in the back garden. Walt first dreamt of amusement parks in the 1930s, but it was not until the 1950s that his obsession developed fully. Amusement parks and circuses at that stage were fairly tacky and disreputable places, and Walt had great difficulty communicating his dream of a place of fun and fantasy in a tidy, orderly setting. His visions went far beyond fairground thrill rides; he wanted *themes* that reinforced his faith in technological progress and the future, a sanitised, deathless world where evil could never triumph, and the archetypal American virtues of pluck and innocence could flourish.

Roy refused to let Walt have the money for Disneyland; he had to cash in his life insurance policy to set it up. But when he turned his attention to Florida there was no such hesitancy about the $5.5 million or so (a mere fleabite to Disney by then) to purchase the land.

EPCOT's Caribbean Beach Resort

Walt had proved his point: his theme parks were a different order of magnitude from anyone else's. They represented his ideal private universe.

The geosphere looms over EPCOT

The Making of Walt Disney World

The founder of this spectacular pleasure park never lived to see it completed. Disney selected the site for three reasons: large tracts of land were available cheaply, the Orlando area was already booming, and it stood at the crossroads of several major traffic arteries. Perhaps, also, the name augured well: Disneyland had prospered in Orange County, California; now here was Orange County, Florida, ripe for picking. Disney deliberately turned his back on Florida's popular coast, but his apparently eccentric decision to put a theme park in the middle of nowhere paid off. Walt wanted people to visit his man-made phenomenon, not be sidetracked by natural wonders such as oceans or mountains or national parks. Quietly, without publicity, the land was purchased on behalf of Disney back in 1964, and the bulldozers soon moved in to hack down the palmetto scrub and build drainage canals. Meanwhile, Walt's ambitions for his brave new world grew like beanstalks; he wanted not merely a theme park or holiday resort, but an entire Utopian city, without slums, poverty or crime – a model of successful planning and innovative lifestyles. Sadly, Disney lost his race against time. Uncle Walt's signature tune, a perpetual smoker's cough, suddenly developed a more sinister note in the spring of 1966, and by the end of the year he was dead. At only 65, he was still full of energy and bursting with ideas for his great Floridian dream, which he mapped out on the ceiling from his hospital bed until the day he died. It was left to his heirs and a new-look Team Disney master-minded by brother Roy to construct Walt Disney World from the blueprint. It finally opened in October 1971. Today it has clones, in Tokyo and Paris. Many visitors refer to WDW simply as 'Disney World', after the Californian prototype Disneyland. Walt's elder brother Roy insisted on giving it the founder's tag ('Walt Disney World') after his death, a generous personal tribute to the man who had ignored all Roy's predictions, and trusted his own instincts. Within the Disney organisation, the name is never shortened to 'Disney World'.

THEME PARK TIPS

A few golden rules for enjoying the action-packed offerings of Orlando. These apply to most of the large theme parks in the area, but particularly to Walt Disney World.

● Plan your visits carefully. You will not make the most of Orlando in a limited time unless you have very clear ideas of what you want to do. Prioritise the things that attract you most. Study the theme park maps and guides (freely available from many sources) like a military exercise; most are very clear and helpful. Check park opening times (they may vary at short notice throughout the year depending on demand). Arrive at the large parks early, and pace yourself for a long day.

● Learn to queue creatively! There is a lot of queuing to do. The parks try their best to entertain you as you wait with video shows on monitors above the lines, but there is no avoiding a lot of hanging about for popular attractions.

● Remember where you leave your car. Note the row number or section name. Write it down. (If you do forget, you will get so mad you will never do it again!) Staff are on hand to help if you really get stuck. Never leave pets in cars – they will fry, for even in January the average temperature is over 22°C (70°F).

● Wear cool, comfortable clothes, especially shoes. Take precautions against the sun, even in winter – the Florida sun is very strong, and some

Those ears get everywhere...

people (particularly children and those with fair skins) can get sunburnt in half an hour or even less. Drink plenty of water.

● Allow time to relax. A non-stop round of theme-parking can be very exhausting, especially for small children. Noise levels within many attractions are high.

● If you leave any of the parks intending to return later in the day, get a hand-stamp of invisible ink at the turnstile.

● Do not prejudge either the parks or the attractions within them. Every one of Orlando's attractions is someone's favourite, and someone's least favourite. You cannot tell whether *you* will enjoy something unless you try it for yourself. The author's opinions of the rides and shows are simply that – the author's opinions.

● Health and safety warnings are posted all over the parks. They naturally err on the side of caution, but should not be ignored.

● Don't forget – you are here to enjoy yourself. Have a nice day!

THEME PARK TIPS

Theme Park Restrictions
In most parks, you are not allowed to do the following:
● Bring your own food or drink
● Enter without wearing a shirt, or without shoes
● Take flash photographs within most attractions
● Smoke in rides or shows, or while queueing for them

● Drink alcohol (specifically in Magic Kingdom)
● Use credit cards at fast-food restaurants (MasterCard, VISA and American Express are acceptable anywhere else).

Theme Park Facilities
Apart from these rules, the big parks are remarkably

accommodating, making it easy for as many people as possible to use them. Among the many facilities available are: wheelchairs and strollers (pushchairs), rentable for a few dollars a day; baby-feeding and changing facilities (disposable nappies, or diapers, available in many shops); facilities for sight- or hearing-impaired visitors; handicapped parking places, staff assistance, and priority within attractions for wheelchair guests; lockers; an efficient lost and found system (including one for children); package pick-up systems for bulky purchases; help with special dietary requirements; kennels; first aid posts; banks; post boxes and stamps; free transport from parking bays to ticket booths, and within or between parks; camera rental; plenty of clean, tidy WCs; public telephones; drinking fountains; information centres, and staff constantly on hand to help with any problems.

Sickness Ratings

Theme parks affect children differently. Many take the thrills completely in their stride; some get hooked on adrenaline and wildly excited; a few get frightened or sick.

None of the rides in any of the parks cause problems for the vast majority of users. Theme park staff do not want you throwing up all over the place, after all, and few rides last long enough for serious queasiness to develop.

However, listed on page 18 are a few things you might avoid if you or your children get nervous on thrill rides or are very susceptible to motion sickness. At any rate make sure the kids are not too full of jelly sandwiches before you start! If you are pregnant, or have a weak heart, back or neck, don't risk the joltier rides. If you are at all concerned, consult your doctor before you go.

Ponce Inlet
New
Smyrna Beach
Edgewater
95 Oak Hill
Canaveral
National
Seashore
Mims
Titusville
John F Kennedy Space Center
Merritt Island NWR
Spaceport USA Visitors Center
Cape Canaveral
Cocoa
Cape Canaveral
Merritt Island
Rockledge
Cocoa Beach
Satellite Beach
Indian Harbour Beach
Indialantic
Melbourne
Palm Bay
Grant
95
Sebastian
Fellsmere
Indian River

THEME PARK TIPS

Without question the wildest rides in Orlando's theme parks are the **Magic Kingdom Space Mountain**. The G-forces are hard on your spine and, because you are in the dark, you cannot predict or brace yourself for the movements. That is why the fans love it! **EPCOT Center Body Wars** is a simulated ride through the human body which some find disturbing as much for its subject matter as for any movement involved. **Disney–MGM Studios Star Tours** is another simulated ride with dizzying visual effects. The **Rock 'n' Rollercoaster** is fast and furious with UV lighting. **Universal Orlando's Back to the Future** and the **Amazing Adventures of Spiderman** are undoubtedly the most 'intense' simulated experiences here.

Wet'n Wild theme park is based on an exciting swimming complex

You'll also find **Duelling Dragons** and the **Incredible Hulk** roller coasters at the **Islands of Adventure**. **Gwazi** completes **Busch Gardens**' trio of spectacular roller coasters (**Kumba** and **Montu** are the other two) and is Florida's first duelling wooden roller coaster and the southeast's largest and fastest wooden coaster. Others to avoid if pregnant or you have a weak heart are the **Congo River Rapids**, the **Tanganyika Tidal Wave**, the **Python, Scorpion** and **Akbar's Adventure Tours**. The **Rhino Rally** can be bumpy. Some people find the **3-D CircleVision** shows (there are several in the EPCOT World Showcase pavilions) mildly disturbing. Nothing actually moves except the pictures on the curved screen, but the illusion of motion is very convincing, hence the rails for you to hold on to.

What to See

Attractions are not always listed in strict alphabetical order under theme park names, but have been arranged by the author into the most useful sequences to best visit and enjoy each ride or show on the ground.

WALT DISNEY WORLD

This enormous resort complex covers some 47 square miles (111 sq km). Within it are four huge theme parks, three water parks, a nightclub theme park, almost 20 hotels (some of which are self-contained themed resorts), a massive campground, a villa complex, five golf-courses, numerous swimming pools and tennis courts, shops, restaurants, beaches, lakes, roads, woods, an impressive network of public transport, and dozens of individual attractions. Less than a quarter of the site has been developed: another quarter is designated a 'wilderness preserve'.

Walt Disney World is constantly being updated and attractions redesigned to keep up with the latest technology. You may therefore find that individual attractions may be closed at one time or another.

Tickets (Passes)

Admission to the Disney parks goes like this:

● **Single-day tickets** are valid for one park only, (Animal Kingdom, EPCOT Center, Magic Kingdom or Disney–MGM Studios). These one day passes are not the best solution if you will be spending more than one day in the resort. Approximately $49 adults, $39 children 3–9.

● A **Hopper Pass** is valid for any park at any time of day. Some include options such as a visit to a water park, Pleasure island or an event at Wild World of Sports. You can choose a **Four-Day Hopper Pass** (approximately $186 adults, $157 children), a **Five-Day Hopper Pass** with two options (approximately $219 adults, $177 children), a **Six-Day Hopper Pass** with three options (approximately $282 adults, $230 children) or a **Seven-Day Hopper Pass** with four options (approximately $314 adults, $257 children).

● For Disney Resort Guests only there is **The Ultimate Park Hopper** (also known as Unlimited Magic)with unlimited admission to theme parks, water parks, nature parks, the sports complex and Pleasure Island (two days and one night approximately $120 adults, $100 children)

Which Pass to Choose?

Many package holidays to central Florida include either a four- or five-day pass to WDW. Presumably if you are considering this area as a holiday destination you will want to see Walt Disney World. If you are spending just a week here and plan to see some of Florida's other attractions, it may be better to take single-day tickets to whichever Disney theme parks interest you most. You can, at a pinch, get a good flavour of each of the big parks in a day, though this will not allow you time to linger in shops or enjoy leisurely lunches.

If you spend longer than a week in Orlando, buy the Five-day Super Pass: the water parks and Pleasure Island are well worth seeing, and provide a relaxing antidote to the pressured activity of the bigger parks.

Opening Hours

The major parks generally stay open long hours, all day, every day of the year. During periods of exceptional crowding they may close if they get full. Precise opening times vary according to seasonal demand, and may change at short notice. Check when you arrive in Orlando at its Visitor Information Center, or direct with WDW (tel: 824 4321); re-check whenever you arrive at the parks. Gates usually open at least half an hour before the official opening time, and it is well worth arriving as early as you can to avoid queues and make the most of your day. Individual attractions close from time to time for technical reasons or for maintenance (equipment safety is constantly monitored), and some special shows take place only when the parks stay open late in the evenings (usually the busiest days, see below). Bad weather rarely affects the large parks, but may close water parks such as Typhoon Lagoon and Blizzard Beach.

Avoiding the Crowds

Busiest days at the Magic Kingdom are generally Monday, Thursday and Saturday, while Animal Kingdom tends to attract crowds in the early part of the week (Monday–Wednesday). Disney–MGM Studios gets most traffic later in the week, from Wednesday to Friday and sometimes Sundays. Finally, try to avoid EPCOT Center on Tuesdays. If the weather is bad, do not cancel your visit; you will be able to enjoy the parks in less crowded conditions (in any case, Florida weather rarely stays gloomy for long). The busiest holiday period is between Christmas and New Year. Thanksgiving weekend and other US holidays, spring break and Easter time are also extremely busy. The parks are quietest from Thanksgiving weekend until the week before Christmas.

Make your first glimpse of Walt Disney World Cinderella's Castle at the Magic Kingdom. The boat ride across the Seven Seas Lagoon is a spellbinding way to start your visit. Tackle EPCOT Center next, as it is the largest and most challenging of the parks.

Travelling within WDW

The size of the Disney site makes it quite impractical to stroll about from park to park, so study a good map and bone up on how to get about. Road systems are very well signed, though they are complex and you will rapidly lose any sense of direction once within the World. Look out for landmarks (each park has one, visible for miles: Cinderella Castle, Spaceship Earth, the Earffel Tower), or hotels (the World Swan and World Dolphin are particularly striking). A car is not essential, but is definitely the most convenient way to get around Walt Disney World. Parking is free if you stay within WDW, otherwise it is about $4 at each theme park. Golden rule: remember where you leave the car! Disney transport is little short of miraculous, but the sheer distances and crowds could delay your arrival time at the parks. Identification may be required on some routes (you are not entitled to use the transport between parks on single-day tickets, but staff sometimes turn a blind eye). Buses are all clearly flagged with different colours – pick up a plan which tells you which one to look out for. One circular loop of the monorail system links the resorts around the Seven Seas Lagoon in the Magic Kingdom with the Transportation and Ticket Center (TTC), and an inner loop travelling anticlockwise provides an express service. A second loop takes you southwards to EPCOT Center (change at TTC). Ferries ply across the lagoons, and through various canals to resort hotels and Disney–MGM Studios.

EPCOT CENTER ✓

The second of WDW's great theme parks opened in October 1982, though Walt had already set the ball rolling shortly before his death in 1966. The name is a contraction of 'Experimental Prototype Community of Tomorrow', a cumbersome appellation that obscures more than it clarifies. The main concept behind this ambitious theme park is to provide a window on the world of new ideas and technologies. Walt Disney's original plans included an entire city with permanent residents and model industries.

EPCOT Center is more than twice the size of the Magic Kingdom, and more serious in tone, straying much further into the domain of education, though some would claim the educational content of EPCOT is fairly superficial. Many children under 10 will appreciate it only in part, and may be frankly bored by some of it. For all that, much of EPCOT is highly entertaining too, and the massive scale of its operations is nothing short of spectacular. Every bit of the park is squeaky clean and beautifully (if sterilely) landscaped with neat gardens, obedient fountains and broad walkways, music pouring from loudspeakers at intervals. EPCOT Center forms a rough figure-of-eight shape, and contains two separate elements: Future World and World Showcase. **Future World**, in the

Spectromagic with Mickey Mouse

The Living Seas exhibition in Future World

bottom ring of the '8', consists of a group of elaborate pavilions devoted to some aspect of modern life. Each pavilion houses a number of multimedia themed attractions. New for 2003, presented by the Compaq Computer Corporation, is **Mission:SPACE**. This galactic adventure will enable guests to experience what it is really like to be an astronaut. The focal landmark of EPCOT Center, visible for miles around, is a silvery geosphere like a massive golf-ball at the entrance to the park, known as **Spaceship Earth**. This unique futuristic structure is made of aluminium and weighs a million pounds (over 450 thousand kilos). When you get disorientated among EPCOT's vast range of attractions, just look for the silver ball.

The upper ring of the '8' is occupied by another of those artificial lakes so beloved by Disney landscapers. Around the edge of the lagoon lies the **World Showcase**, a group of pavilions depicting aspects of 11 different countries. Collectively this attraction forms something not unlike a world trade fair, each nation promoting itself through its products, cuisine and tourist potential.

Practical Details

To see absolutely everything at EPCOT you need longer than a day; however, it is unlikely you will be equally fascinated by all of it, and you can skim sections quickly if they do not interest you much. EPCOT's delights are envisaged as dynamic rather than static. New attractions and ideas are constantly being added, and obsolete ones withdrawn, so you may find things not as described below. The same excellent guest facilities are available as in the other parks. All around EPCOT you will see WorldKey interactive video terminals offering touch-screen information and advice about the park facilities. You can even call up a real-live attendant to answer your questions on this two-way system ('How may I help you? Please don't be shy!'). One of the highlights of any EPCOT visit is the closing show called IllumiNations, a spectacular display of lasers, fireworks and coloured fountains, over the Showcase Lagoon, when all the pavilions around the lagoon light up to music in turn. One of the best spots to watch the show from is Mexico's Cantina de San Angel – get there early though as tables cannot be reserved.

Future World

♦♦
SPACESHIP EARTH

Nobody can fail to notice the massive golf ball-like structure of this ride at the entrance to EPCOT.
Inside the vast silver dome is a time-machine ride past animated tableaux depicting the achievements of humankind through the ages, from prehistoric cave dwellers to the space age. Queues can be very long. If so, try later in the day. At the base of the geosphere is **Earth Station**, EPCOT's main information and guest relations centre.

♦
INNOVENTIONS

Innoventions exhibits new electrical gadgets, prototypes of the sort of thing that in the future will become part of our everyday living. There are opportunities to step into a house of the future, visit cyber-space and test new developments in information technology.

THE LIVING SEAS

Most visitors find this pavilion extremely entertaining and well presented. You descend in a marvellously futuristic diving ship to Sea Base Alpha, a fine aquarium exhibit with massive tanks and lots of tropical fish in a Florida reef setting. In the attractive and popular Coral Reef Restaurant you can gawp at fish, and eat them at the same time.

♦♦♦
THE LAND

An interesting pavilion devoted to food and agriculture. Needless to say, there is plenty to eat here, and it gets full of folk chomping chocolate cake around lunchtime. Other things to do include: **Listen to the Land**, a boatride through various inhospitable

On the Journey into Imagination

ecosystems, and a futuristic greenhouse using latest plant technology; **Food Rock** is an amusing AudioAnimatronic rock concert; and **Harvest Theater**, showing a worthy film called *Symbiosis* about people and the environment.
This is one of the most interesting of EPCOT's presentations. Plant lovers who want more after the green-house boat tour can sign up for an hour–long 'Behind the Seeds' guided walk, which explores the futuristic greenhouses in more depth.

◆◆
JOURNEY INTO IMAGINATION
The Imagination Institute has been renovated and updated. Inside you will find *Honey, I Shrunk the Audience*, a 25–minute 3–D presentation that begins with a brief pre-show

before you step inside to watch Professor Wayne Szalinski, star of *Honey, I Shrunk the Kids*, receive an award for and demonstrate his latest invention. Warning: do not sit at the front for this – the effects do not work well at close range. **Image Works** involves lots of participatory stuff with electronic paintbrushes and an orchestra you conduct by waving your hands over a console. Greatest fun at this pavilion are the **Jumping Fountains** outside, which keep visitors goggling in amazement as disembodied, apparently solid arcs of water leap from one pool to another.

◆◆◆
TEST TRACK
After seeing how new cars are tested on banked curves, high-speed curves, with special brakes, without special brakes,

over bumpy roads and in crash tests, you board a six-passenger vehicle (minus a steering wheel and brakes) and experience what you just saw. There are 65–mph straight runs, hairpin bends, near–collisions and everything necessary to make this the most exciting attraction at EPCOT.

WONDERS OF LIFE
A large pavilion housing several entertaining multimedia presentations relating to health and the human body. In the concourse you can measure your fitness on exercise machines and eat 'health' foods (chocolate milkshakes?). **Body Wars** is a jolty flight-simulated ride through the human body. **Cranium Command** is an excellent and very funny AudioAnimatronic show about the human brain. **The Making of Me** is pretty daring stuff for Disney – a film about sex (human reproduction, if you prefer). It is tastefully done and not at all embarrassing, engagingly presented by a boy speculating about where he came from. True to the Disney ethos, the participants fall in love and get married first.

UNIVERSE OF ENERGY
This extravagant presentation by the Exxon company is not to be missed. It is a truly remarkable ride in a huge travelling theatre. First you watch an animated film on fossil fuels (sharp intake of breath at shots of Port Valdise and Arctic pipelines). Then the seats split up and trundle off on an odyssey through a prehistoric forest with terrific dinosaurs and thunderstorms. It even smells of dank vegetation.

World Showcase
The World Showcase does not open until 11AM. To beat the crowds, be next door in The Land or Journey into the imagination at this time. It does not matter which direction you take around the Showcase – however, anti-clockwise can be less crowded earlier in the day. All the pavilions have some sort of appropriately themed architectural motif, one or more typical restaurant, shops selling national products, and

Sunshine reflected from the golden dome, the Wonders of Life pavilion

The China pavilion

sometimes live entertainment, film shows or other attractions.

◆◆
CANADA
Totem poles and a Canadian landscape of rocky canyons and waterfalls set the scene for *O Canada!*, a CircleVision film about Mounties and other national glories. Le Cellier is a cafeteria-style restaurant.

◆
UNITED KINGDOM
The centrepiece Rose and Crown pub is among what looks like a curious amalgam of Hyde Park, the Cotswolds and Edinburgh. You can buy Bass bitter here. Shops sell Pringle woollies, Twinings tea, Royal Doulton china, and Crabtree & Evelyn cosmetics.

◆◆
FRANCE
Mansard roofs and a mini-Eiffel Tower pinpoint one of the best restaurants (*mais naturellement*) in the World Showcase, and lots of mouth-watering shops.
Impressions de France whirls visitors through undefined Gallic landscapes to French

music. Camera effects are very impressive.

◆◆
MOROCCO
One of the most distinctive pavilions architecturally: a walled desert city with minarets and carved gateways. Belly-dancing goes on over couscous in the Marrakesh restaurant, and many traditional crafts are on display in the *medina*.

◆
JAPAN
Beautiful landscaping, the Bijutsu-kan Gallery, a Mitsukoshi Department Store, and several restaurants characterise this pagoda complex.

◆◆◆
THE AMERICAN ADVENTURE
This takes centre stage, of course, involving an elaborately constructed replica of Philadelphia's Liberty Hall. The patriotic AudioAnimatronics show within is well worth seeing and lasts a stirring 29 minutes, with Ben Franklin and Mark Twain presiding over the historical production.

◆◆
ITALY
St Mark's Square sets the scene for Italian luxury goods and spaghetti, with live entertainment at the Teatro di Bologna.

◆◆
GERMANY
The main attraction is the Biergarten with traditional Germanic entertainment (oompah music) and folk-dancing in a setting of Grimm's Fairy Tale architecture. Souvenirs include lovely Hummel figurines.

Mickey keeps an eye on his guests

CHINA
A fine CircleVision film, *The Wonders of China*, is worth catching here. The restaurant is very pricey, but there are lots of souvenirs to buy.

NORWAY
With a 14th–century castle, Akerhus; a gift shop filled with trolls; a restaurant, and **The Maelstrom** – a boat ride through a troll-filled forest and the raging North Sea.

MEXICO
One of the most exciting pavilions visually, marked by pre-Columbian pyramids and exotic carvings. **El Rio del Tiempo** is an exciting boat ride through the ancient cultures of Central America, a fine if somewhat censored exhibition of art, some beautiful jewellery and a very pleasant restaurant, the San Angel.

THE MAGIC KINGDOM ✓

The Magic Kingdom is what most people think of when Walt Disney World is mentioned. This giant play-pen of fairies, monsters, and those immortal cartoon characters Mickey Mouse and friends, was the first section of WDW to be constructed, and is modelled closely on the original Disneyland theme park in California. Covering 100 acres (40 ha) with nearly 60 major attractions, it is on a larger scale than its Californian parent, and crowding is less intense. The focal point of the Magic Kingdom is **Cinderella Castle**, a dreamy mass of spires and turrets visible from many parts of the park.

Practical Details
When you have parked and arrived at the ticket booths to

the Magic Kingdom, you still have some way to go. To reach the attractions you must take either a monorail journey, or the ferry across the **Seven Seas Lagoon**. The ferry ride gives you the best view of Cinderella Castle, and allows child-like anticipation to build up nicely. Seen from a distance like a mirage across the Lagoon, the castle looks magical indeed. The Magic Kingdom is divided into seven different 'lands' arranged round an island between **Main Street, USA** and Cinderella Castle known as the **Central Plaza**. These lands are Main Street USA, Adventureland, Frontierland, Liberty Square, Fantasyland, Mickey's Toontown Fair and New Tomorrowland. Most people naturally seem to tackle them clockwise from Main Street (the order in which they appear below), but if you duck and dive you may miss some of the queues. The main attractions are briefly outlined below, but throughout the park there are dozens of sideshows, shops and eating places to distract you, and what seems a continuous barrage of live entertainment: parades, stunts, marching bands, musicians and, of course, the cartoon characters wandering about ready to fascinate the kids and pose for endless photographs. Best of these diversions are the **Three o'clock Parade** (daily at 15:00hrs; best viewing point is Frontierland), and the wonderful night shows: **Spectromagic**, with over 30 dazzling floats, the firework show **Fantasy in the Sky**, and the **Floating Electrical Pageant** on Seven Seas Lagoon

(visible from the Contemporary or Polynesian Resorts). These shows are extremely spectacular, but take place only when the park stays open late (peak season and some weekends). It is worth choosing a day when they happen for your visit to the Magic Kingdom. Check in advance. When you arrive, visit guest relations to pick up a map and check the times and locations of parades and character appearances. There is also a board at the top of Main Street which advises guests of the queuing times for rides. To save on queuing time, make use of the **FASTPASS** system. You are issued with a time slot in which you can return and 'jump the queue'.

Main Street USA

This is the hub of the Magic Kingdom from which the other lands radiate, and Cinderella's castle is its focus. With more than a hint of Mad King Ludwig of Bavaria's turreted folly Neuschwanstein, this 180–foot steel and fibreglass fantasy castle encapsulates the park's storybook allure. Main Street recreates a pristine Victorian village of 'olde worlde' shopfronts and colour-coordinated floral displays, barbershop quartets, ice-cream parlours and hot dog stands with striped awnings. The shops are tempting but don't linger too long when you first arrive, leave them for later when you exit the park, the atmosphere after the fireworks is wonderful – and you won't have to carry or collect bags.

WALT DISNEY RAILROAD
A beautiful narrow-gauge steam train journey around the Magic Kingdom. There are stations in Frontierland and Mickey's Toontown Fair as well as Main Street USA.

Adventureland
Several excellent attractions here in varied tropical settings, all worth catching, and some appealing souvenirs and ice-creams.

SWISS FAMILY TREEHOUSE
A splendid den. Now is that banyan tree real, or not? It is not until you are high up in the leafy branches that the illusion cracks – only the dripping Spanish moss is genuine. Lots of steps to climb, and it can be a slow shuffle round the duckboards to see the homey rooms.

JUNGLE CRUISE
An enjoyable if geographically faithless voyage through Amazon rainforests, the Nile valley, and a Southeast Asian jungle. Lots of animals on the way, and gas heaters concealed in the rocks to step up the temperatures.

PIRATES OF THE CARIBBEAN
A great adventure cruise following Audio-Animatronic technology pirates. En route you pass elaborately constructed sets of wrecks, raids and castaways, some quite alarming for young children. All accompanied by appropriate music.

ENCHANTED TIKI BIRDS – UNDER NEW MANAGEMENT
An enjoyable and funny show where you can relax in a thatched hut and enjoy hundreds of animated singing birds, flowers and tribal totems. Suitable for all ages.

THE MAGIC CARPETS OF ALADDIN
A gentle flying experience in a mystic land, with controls to raise and lower your carpet while circling the Genie's lamp.

Frontierland
Pioneer magic with an Old West flavour.

BIG THUNDER MOUNTAIN RAILROAD
An exhilarating but not too terrifying roller-coaster ride through Arizona scenery and an old mining set where a mini-rockfall assails you. The journey is too fast to take in all the elaborate details of the ride, so it is one you could well do more than once.

SPLASH MOUNTAIN
With a 50-ft drop at 40-mph you can't fail to find this flume thrilling. Based on animated sequences in Walt Disney's 1946 film *Song of the South*, the ride follows the adventures of Brer Rabbit, Bear and Fox.

TOM SAWYER ISLAND
A pleasant, though not wildly

The night show Fantasy in the Sky is a special attraction

exciting, outdoor attraction reached by raft, based on Tom and Huck's adventures, with scary caves, mock forts and barrel bridges. Aunt Polly's Landing is a good place to relax with peanut butter and jelly sandwiches and watch the paddle-steamer cruise by.

◆◆
COUNTRY BEAR VACATION HOEDOWN

Corny but relentlessly engaging show with foot-stompin' animated bears and singing mooseheads. It is cleverly done and very raucous.

◆◆
DIAMOND HORSESHOE JAMBOREE

Enthusiastic, cheerful Western dance-hall show held several times a day. Note: reservations are usually needed, and you can book a place at the Diamond Horseshoe itself.

Liberty Square

Clapboard architecture and tidy gardens evoke an ambience of Yankee respectability and national pride. The **Liberty Tree**, a symbolic live oak recalling Boston Tea Party days, forms a focal point among the shops selling pricey 'antiques' and American heritage souvenirs. This is a pleasant place to relax on shady benches, have lunch at the Liberty Tree Tavern, or take a leisurely boat cruise in the heat of the day on the three-decker riverboat. Smaller **Mickey Fink Keel Boats** ply the same stretches of water. There are two very different attractions in this 'land'.

◆◆
HALL OF PRESIDENTS

Cleverly done in its way, though it is hardly a barrel of laughs.

The Haunted Mansion

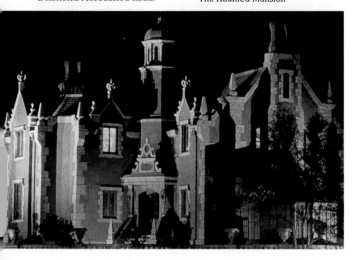

Visitors get a basinful of the US Constitution, a rapid gallop through the Civil War, a flourish of the Stars and Stripes, and a reminder of the American Dream (lest we forget) from Abe Lincoln. The show includes a roll-call of US presidents, all carefully attired in correct period costume, and shuffling animatronically from time to time.

HAUNTED MANSION
Entertaining and mostly hilarious. Only the very susceptible will get any serious frights aboard this cobwebby ghost train and its 999 'happy haunts'. Transparent spectres whirl in a *danse macabre*, suits of armour clank into action, and a persistent raven hovers.

Fantasyland
In the shadow of the fairy-tale castle lies a collection of themed attractions ranging from the fictions of J M Barrie to Jules Verne. Older children may scorn simple fairground fun like **Dumbo the Flying Elephant**, the **Mad Tea Party** and **Cinderella's Golden Carousel**, but tinies love them. Fantasyland is understandably popular with the younger set and is consequently often crowded. Not all the rides repay the long waits.

IT'S A SMALL WORLD
Saccharine and schmaltzy, but the special effects are remarkable. It's a long boat ride through cavern after cavern of elaborately animated dolls, a medley of light and

movement and infuriating tunes.

PETER PAN'S FLIGHT
Enjoyable, gentle journey through the sky suspended from an overhead rail.

LEGEND OF THE LION KING
If you liked the film, you'll enjoy this show which combines film clips, puppetry and live-costumed actors in a 25–minute show. Songs from the fantastic soundtrack are performed and there is a pre-show given by Raffiki to set the scene. Keep little ones close as the show is true to the film, including Mufassa's death.

◆
SNOW WHITE'S SCARY ADVENTURES
The wicked queen tries to blight everyone's life. Not really all that scary.

◆
THE MANY ADVENTURES OF WINNIE THE POOH
Hop aboard your 'hunny pot' for a cuddly, honey-laden trip to the Hundred Acre Wood to visit Pooh, Piglet, Owl and Eeyore.

Disneymania
If the kids tire of rides there is Disneymania – live singing and dancing shows with Mickey and the gang – which takes place in front of Cinderella Castle.

Mickey's Toontown Fair
Originally a temporary addition, this section of the park was so popular it earnt 'permanent' status. A popular photo-stop with its colourful, out-size surroundings

WALT DISNEY WORLD: THE MAGIC KINGDOM

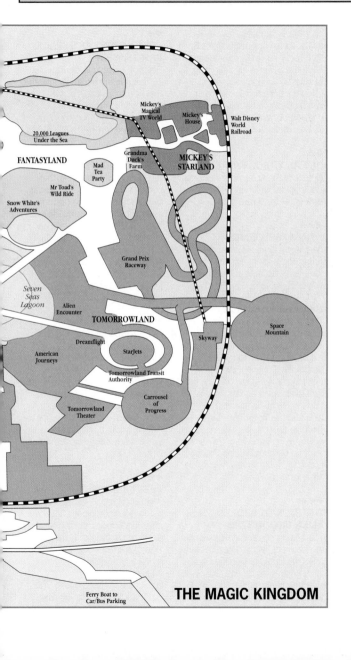

and Disney topiary, Toontown offers a rare opportunity to visit the world's most famous mouse 'at home'. Take a stroll around Mickey's Country House and Minnie's Country House, then catch up with favourite Disney cartoon characters at the Toontown hall of Fame.

DONALD'S BOAT PLAY AREA
A watery fun area where hot tots can cool off and burn off excess energy at the same time.

THE BARNSTORMER
A scaled-down roller coaster designed especially for children, situated at Goofy's Wiseacres Farm.

New Tomorrowland
The cone-shaped pavilion housing Tomorrowland's star attraction vies with Cinderella's castle as a Magic Kingdom landmark. Fantasy-orientated New Tomorrowland offers a full complement of escapist rides and antagonistic aliens. You'll also find the **Tomorrowland Arcade** (not the best place to go unless you're made of money) and the **Galaxy Palace Theater**, home to several variety shows and performances.

THE EXTRATERRORESTRIAL ALIEN ENCOUNTER
This sensory chiller, designed with the help of George Lucas, really does raise the hairs on the back of your neck, with a combination of special effects, suggestion and short periods of total darkness. Certainly an experience.

BUZZ LIGHTYEAR'S SPACE RANGER SPIN
Blast off from Star Command Headquarters on an interactive mission to defeat the evil Zurg and his minions. Passengers get to test their laser shooting skills.

SPACE MOUNTAIN
A terrific roller coaster that rockets through the darkness past meteors and shooting stars. This is a rough ride, so batten down the hatches and take off. The queuing adds to the anticipation of the ride and is an experience in itself. Once you've passed the point of no return all you can do is scream.

CAROUSEL OF PROGRESS
After the thrills of Space Mountain, this gentler attraction may wind you down. The Carousel of Progress is one of the Magic Kingdom's most popular attractions and Tomorrowland just wouldn't be right without this 'cheesy' ride through one hundred years of a family's life.

THE TIMEKEEPER
A great place to kill two birds with one stone - get another attraction under your belt and get a sit down! For light relief, visit The Timekeeper, hosted by a jocular, Robin Williams voiced robot and his flighty sidekicks, which whisks you back and forth through time to meet famous inventors

Space Mountain

and visionaries in Circle Vision 360.

◆
TOMORROWLAND TRANSIT AUTHORITY

Previously called Wedway Peoplemover, this ponderous ride in a linear induction-powered mass transportation system (any the wiser?) gives you a chance to decide you do not like the look of Space Mountain, but not much else. Environmentally, though, it is all edifying stuff.

◆
TOMORROWLAND SPEEDWAY

Sponsored by Goodyear, this is a popular ride with children. Its mini racing cars race around four 2,260–foot tracks at not–so–fast top speeds!

◆
ASTRO ORBITERS

A rocket ride with a good view of New Tomorrowland. Only really worth doing with children or if there isn't a queue.

DISNEY–MGM STUDIOS ✓

Opened in 1989, MGM provides a showcase for the huge range of Disney TV and film productions, which now cater for adults as well as children. The Walt Disney Company has obtained rights to use the weighty name and productions of Metro–Goldwyn–Mayer to illuminate more than half a century of motion-picture making. Disney-MGM Studios re-creates the aura of heyday Hollywood from the 1930s onwards, as those of us who were never there like to imagine it. Against a backdrop of Art Deco sets and yesteryear automobiles, visitors find many of today's screen celebrities brought to life with the latest technology and dramatic special effects, from Muppets to Indiana Jones. Needless to say, Mickey Mouse is remembered too, most noticeably in Disney– MGM's most striking landmark, the Earffel Tower (a water tower near the main entrance crowned with those unmistakable round black ears)

Practical Details

The immense popularity of Disney–MGM Studios took Disney planners by surprise, and since the park first opened it has expanded greatly, with many plans afoot for further attractions. Still very much a working TV and film studio; large parts of it are off-limits or accessible only by guided tour. Crowding can be a problem at times. As in the other parks, it is advisable to arrive early (particularly for **the big rides**) It is the most southerly of the theme parks, well signed from the Maingate entrance. There is parking for 4,500 vehicles, with tram transport to the ticket booths, and lots of buses ply regularly to other parts of WDW. You can also reach Disney–MGM Studios by boat from the EPCOT Center resort hotels. Within the park you get around mostly on foot, though the backstage tour includes a tram ride. Several attractions, however, involve lengthy sit-downs for films and shows, so there are plenty of chances to rest your feet in the shade. Shops, restaurants, and all the usual Disney facilities for visitors can be found at the Studios. Among the usual mass-produced range of Disneyana clutter, you can find more genuine reminders of why Walt Disney is a household name, such as original animation 'cels' – drawings for the early cartoons. In addition to the main attractions and regular shows that go on all day, look out for constant music and entertainment in the 'streets'. **The Hollywood Boulevard Parade** takes place at 3PM and is usually themed to Disney's latest film. When the park stays open late, a fireworks and laser show called **Fantasmic!** takes place at the end of the day. Disney characters appear with singers and dancers in musical cabaret shows in the **Theater of the Stars**. Pick up a schedule of special events from the **Production Information Window** as you enter the park.

◆◆◆
THE GREAT MOVIE RIDE

At the top of Hollywood Boulevard is a full-sized replica of Hollywood's famous **Chinese Theater**, which houses the Studios' first major attraction. It is popular, and you may have quite a wait, but make sure you see it at some stage during your visit. This elaborate multimedia ride through sound-stage sets from many classic Hollywood greats is a real *tour de force*, and one of the biggest and most ambitious attractions within WDW. On your tram ride you will encounter over a hundred extraordinarily realistic models, including James Cagney, John Wayne, Gene Kelly, Julie Andrews and Harrison Ford. To add spice to the adventure, your train will be ambushed by bank robbers and threatened by a hideous Alien before passing into the more romantic climes of *Casablanca* and *The Wizard of Oz*.

◆◆◆
THE TWILIGHT TOWER OF TERROR

Seated in an elevator you will drift through a mysterious dimension in this grand hotel, struck by lightning in 1939, from which a whole section of the building and five people in a lift disappeared. A door opens and you see the park 150 feet below. Then the doors close, the cable breaks and your car plunges straight down. Its scary to say the least, but you'll want to do it again!

Encounters on the Great Movie Ride

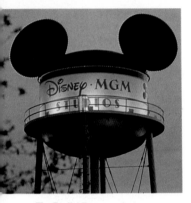

The Earffel Tower at dusk

◆◆◆
ROCK 'N' ROLLER COASTER STARRING AEROSMITH

Fronted by a giant red electric guitar, this roller coaster takes the form of a motorised dash across town to catch an Aerosmith concert. After boarding the Limotrain, guests are launched from 0–60mph in 2.8 seconds and reach forces of 5Gs. Mega thrills and great soundtrack from the old rockers themselves.

◆◆
BEAUTY AND THE BEAST – LIVE ON STAGE

A 20–minute performance that captures the essence of the animated film. Its a terrific stage show that stars singing silverware, a beautiful Belle and a thrilling finale.

◆◆◆
BACKSTAGE STUDIO TOUR

Again, not to be missed. Takes you through an actual working studio. Highlights of the long but fast-paced and always entertaining tram tour include **Catastrophe Canyon**, where an impressive earthquake and a flash flood are staged for your delight. (Protect your camera if you sit on the left.) You get to see literally 'behind the scenes' of those realistic-looking Hollywood villas used for suburban shots (they are mere shells at the back), inspect the costume, lighting and props departments, and discover how those elaborately painted trick-perspective Manhattan flats can be readily adapted for Anytown USA. Second stage of the tour is on foot through **Roger Rabbit's Looney Bin** shop to a special effects tank where you can see how a naval battle and a storm at sea can be filmed in a duckpond, and a hapless audience participant gets drenched. Towards the end of the tour you watch a short film recounting Bette Middler's crazy adventures with a winning lottery ticket. This pacy little number was entirely produced at the Studios; the convincing special effects are fully explained.

The **Post-Production** section investigates the mysteries of sound, computer effects and editing, and is worth seeing. To catch everything working, this tour is best taken after 13.00hrs.

◆◆
BACKSTAGE PASS

A walk-through tour that kicks off with an introduction to animatronic animals, using examples from *101 Dalmations*. Volunteers help illustrate 'bluescreen' editing techniques and then continue past sound stages containing sets from recent and current films and TV shows. Finally, see costumes, props and detailed designers' sketches from *101 Dalmations*.

THE MAGIC OF DISNEY ANIMATION

This is splendid, featuring an unlikely but hilarious combination of Robin Williams and Walter Cronkite in a film about the basic techniques of animation. Afterwards, visitors troop through the animation studios to peer over the shoulders of Disney's huge team of artists, working through storyboards and rough pencil sketches to painstakingly coloured finished artwork. Computers help these days, but a surprising amount of cartoon work still involves the time-honoured hand-drawn method of figures replicated thousands of times on individual 'cels'. How much of the technology you absorb in one circuit is up to you, but you can always have another shot at it if you like.

INDIANA JONES EPIC STUNT SPECTACULAR

A popular and, as the title suggests, exciting show demonstrating professional stunts (some of them highly dangerous) in an adventure movie. Members of the audience volunteer as extras and come in for a fair amount of ridicule, but it is very enjoyable and very watchable. It is also one of the few shows in WDW where you are allowed to take photographs or use camcorders.

STAR TOURS

This space simulation flight includes some of WDW's most amazing visual special effects. If they get too intense, you can always shut your eyes. You should not miss it, but take the health warnings seriously. The crash landing through New York's skyscrapers is definitely not for plane phobics. The techniques and sensations are very similar to those used in the attraction called Body Wars at EPCOT Center. If you can cope with one, you will probably be all right on the other.

MUPPETVISION 3-D

Even if the Muppets are not on your favourite TV-character list, this musical show is highly entertaining and may well win you over. Since Muppet creator Jim Henson's untimely death, the precise terms of Disney's contract with the Muppets have been the subject of an acrimonious dispute, and how much longer the Muppets will grace WDW is anyone's guess. But if they are still there, make sure you see the show.

◆

HONEY I SHRUNK THE KIDS MOVIE SET ADVENTURE

Young children may find this walk-through adventure playground with everything scaled up to Brobdignagian proportions entertaining, but for many people this attraction is one of the weaker and less convincing.

DISNEY–MGM STUDIOS THEME PARK

Earffel Tower

BACKSTAGE STUDIO TOUR

Walt Disney Theater

Backstage Shuttle Station

The Magic of Disney Animation

Twilight Zone Tower of Terror

DISNEY'S ANIMAL KINGDOM ✓

Disney's latest theme park showcases more than 200 animal species in magnificently re-created naturalistic habitats, and combines its zoological role with a strong eco-educational message. You will have to see it at the animals' pace, so adjust your schedule accordingly. It really does pay to make an early start at Disney's Animal Kingdom as the animals are more active in the cooler part of the day. To make your time go further use the FASTPASS system which operates for **Kilamanjaro Safaris**, **Kali River Rapids** and **DINOSAUR!**

The park is divided into two major sections; **Asia** and **Africa**. Other lands include **The Oasis**, **Safari Village**, **DinoLand USA** and **Camp Minnie-Mickey**.

The Oasis

An area of trees and waterfalls, this is Disney's way of telling you to slow down. You'll hear flutes, steel drums and waterfalls and see banana trees, exotic birds and rare plants – let it relax you.

At work in the animation studios

Safari Village

The centrepiece is the **Tree of Life**, a 145–foot–tall symbol for the park, adorned with 325 animals carved into its twisting branches, roots and giant trunk. Follow the **Safari Village Trails** for a close up view of the tree.

IT'S TOUGH BEING A BUG

A fantastic 3–D insect's eye-view of the world. You could see this dozens of times and still not get enough – its that good. Sit near the back for the full effect.

Africa

In the African-inspired Harambe village even the ice-creams come with an imprint of Simba's paw and this is the starting point for some serious wildlife spotting. Along the **Pangani Forest Exploration Trail** there is a close-up look at hippos and meerkats, and a wonderfully lush and misty gorilla habitat. **The Wildlife Express to Conservation Station** is a train ride around the 'backlot' where the animals take a break from their public duties.

CONSERVATION STATION

Peek into the vetinary suite and hatchery and learn how the conservation battle continues on behalf of endangered creatures from Siberian tigers to bluefin tuna.

KILAMANJARO SAFARIS

Africa's top attraction. The safari lorry journey through the African veldt reveals lions, giraffes, wildebeest, rhinos and more. You need to be quick when taking photographs as the driver can't stop for your pictures. Regardless, its a fun – sometimes scary – trip.

Asia

An imaginatively re-created rain forest is the setting for this attractive rural village scenario, complete with rickshaws and ornately hand-painted and decorated Indian trucks.

MAHARAJA JUNGLE TREK

Takes visitors on a stroll around 'ancient' temple ruins, past a bat colony, tapirs and tigers and through aviaries.

KALI RIVER RAPIDS

Stow your valuables in the not-so-waterproof area in the middle of the circular raft and set off on an exciting white-water rafting experience. You will get wet!

DinoLand USA

A 40–foot *Brachiosaurus* skeleton, known as the Oldengate Bridge, spans the entrance to DinoLand USA, where things get distinctly prehistoric.

DINOSAUR!

Board a jeep-like vehicle to travel back in time for a look at the dinosaur era three minutes before the meteorites strike! The mission is to bring back a live dinosaur and there are all sorts of thrills, spills and meteorite showers along the way – a real scream.

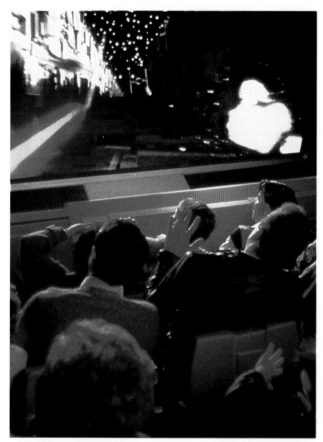

Camp Minnie–Mickey

This frontier-style stockade is great for little kids, with character-greeting area inhabitants including Mickey, Minnie, Goofy plus characters from *The Lion King* and *The Jungle Book*.

◆◆◆
FESTIVAL OF THE LION KING

This is easily the liveliest and most colourful stage show in the

The amazing special effects of Star Tours are not for the faint-hearted!

park – a high-energy song, dance and acrobatic spectacular featuring specialist acts such as fire-jugglers and stilt walkers.

◆
POCAHONTAS AND HER FOREST FRIENDS

Aimed firmly at junior visitors, with plenty of cute animals.

OTHER ATTRACTIONS IN WALT DISNEY WORLD

After you have exhausted the possibilities of the four big theme parks of the Magic Kingdom, EPCOT Center, Disney–MGM Studios, and Disney's Animal Kingdom, there is still plenty else to detain you at Walt Disney World. Check the validity rules of your ticket for entrance regulations.

◆◆
DOWNTOWN DISNEY
WDW Resort's mega shopping, dining and entertainment district on the shores of Lake Buena Vista, Downtown Disney is divided into three parts.

Water-chutes in River Country sweep down into Bay Lake

The **Marketplace** is home to the steaming volcano housing the Rainforest Café, World of Disney – the largest Disney store on earth, and a variety of restaurants and shops. Between the Marketplace and West Side you will find Pleasure Island (see below).

West Side is home to another assortment of fabulous shops, celebrity restaurants and entertainments.

◆◆
PLEASURE ISLAND
Connected to the rest of Downtown Disney by footbridges, Pleasure Island is WDW Resort's offshore home of late-night entertainment, though its shops and restaurants are open all day. The island harbours eight clubs offering a

whole range of musical styles, discos and comedy, plus the West End Stage that occasionally lures top-name talent to the Disney empire, and a New Year's Eve party every night from 11.45PM.

RIVER COUNTRY
This water park in Bay Cove conjures up an archetypal American dream: Huck Finn's perfect swimming hole, a place of prelapsarian innocence in completely (well, almost) natural surroundings. In fact, River Country is a painstaking piece of engineering, with rocky mountain landscapes scarcely native to central Florida, rope swings and flume rides, chutes, pools, fountains and rapids, all plunging round one of the biggest swimming pools hereabouts, a carefully filtered and walled-off section of **Bay Lake**. Quieter types may prefer the white-sand beaches and nature walks through cypress swamps, or just messing about in any of a dozen types of watercraft for hire on the lake. Bass fishing trips can be arranged.
Open: 10.00–17.00hrs, with extended hours in summer and holidays.

TYPHOON LAGOON
The largest and most beautiful water park in Orlando, a lovely place to unwind if all those rides are getting a bit much. The wrecked shrimp boat precariously perched on a man-made mountain, and the windswept rakishness of the park buildings suggest a turbulent time. The well-tended park covers 56 acres (23 ha), its prize central feature a splendid surf lagoon with four-foot (1.2m) waves (which calm down at intervals). Lifeguards are on duty in all the watery places. Scale **Mount Mayday** for a dare on **Humunga Kowabunga** where speeds of up to 25mph can be reached. Three storm slides take a less hair-raising route down to pools around the lagoon. There are also three white water raft adventures. Try the **Shark Reef** and snorkel with harmless versions of Jaws. Hop on a tube and drift on **Castaway Creek** beneath a misty rainforest and through caves.
Open: daily 10.00–17.00hrs, with extended hours in season. Note: in bad weather the Typhoon Lagoon may be closed.

BLIZZARD BEACH
The third park, Blizzard Beach, bizzarely recreates a ski resort, with snow-capped mountains. The park follows the same formula as the others by featuring a large wave pool, a slow river ride and areas for kids. The highlight here is **Summit Plummet**, a 60mph water slide. **Teamboat Springs** is fun in a different, less invasive way, as you get to sit inside a five-person raft as you speed down a 1,200–foot series of waterfalls.
Open: 10.00–17.00hrs, with extended hours in season. May close in bad weather.

SEAWORLD ✓

You cannot spend any time at all in Orlando before realising that Mickey Mouse has a great rival for the affections of sentimental animal-lovers. Worse news for Mickey, this animal is real. Sea World's improbable star exhibit is a killer whale called Shamu. Although several killer whales have been born at Sea World, when Shamu gave birth in 1989 her adoring public fell into raptures. Film footage of the last few minutes of this extraordinary labour are endlessly recycled on video screens throughout the theme park. Shamu makes several graceful pirouettes, then torpedoes her 7-foot (2.1m) long baby half-way across the enormous aquarium. After two seconds of surprise at this abrupt entry into the world (can killer whales blink?), Baby Namu is swimming perfectly, effortlessly, next to momma. Lovely stuff for the marketing men! Shamu's distinctive black and white shape is now SeaWorld's emblem, logo, and principal crowd-puller. SeaWorld is one of the Busch Entertainment Corporation's theme parks, owned by Anheuser–Busch, the brewers who bring you Budweiser and Michelob (there is a working brewery on site). It is undoubtedly one of Orlando's major attractions, and most people seem to love it, whatever their reservations about keeping large sea mammals in captivity. It is obviously a sensitive issue, as indicated by SeaWorld's painstaking, backward-bending attempts to emphasise to all comers their sincere commitment to conservation, education, and research. Certainly the conditions in which SeaWorld's exhibits are housed seem very comfortable, however cramping a mere five million gallons (over 22 million litres) of man-made sea water must seem after the freedom of the ocean.

Anthropomorphists untroubled by any understanding of animal conditioning may assert that a bored or discontented Shamu would simply yawn and swallow at a gulp the daring trainers who romp with her. But how happy Shamu really is must remain a mystery, for unlike sharks, whose fearful teeth are clamped permanently in an attitude of moronic viciousness, the jaws of whales seem to form benevolent, intelligent smiles. How comforting for us!

Practical Details

SeaWorld is well signposted and easy to find, near the intersection of Highway I-4 and the Beeline Expressway (Exit 27A). There is a large free parking lot, which is served by a free tram service to the entrance. SeaWorld is one of the largest marine parks in the world and it is advisable to arrive when the gates open, and plan your morning exploration around the show times. These are sensibly scheduled so that, if you move fairly sharply between one and the next, you can see all the

On the Typhoon Lagoon

saying 'Thank you for visiting us. Making friends is our business.' *Open:* year-round 09.00–19.00hrs (later in summer and at holiday times). Some of the main attractions are listed below, but new shows are being planned all the time.

◆◆
TERRORS OF THE DEEP
This attraction provides a scary cast of barracudas, sharks and razor-toothed Moray eels which can be viewed from a plexiglass tunnel through the 660,000–gallon shark tank.

◆◆◆
PENGUIN ENCOUNTER
This is delightful. Several species of these comical creatures live in apparent harmony in what seems to be a fair attempt at a natural habitat. Snow and ice fall from the skylights, and mini-glaciers tumble down the rocks. Through their glazed enclosure you can see the penguins moving both on land and below the waterline, when they look quainter than any Disney animation. The second half of this attraction displays the Arctic cousins of the penguins: puffins and auks. If anything, these are even more appealing, scudding about like small robots.

◆◆
SEA LION AND OTTER SHOW
A silly but quite funny and even mildly educative show featuring waddling sea lions, a cheeky otter, and a splendidly hideous walrus.

attractions quite efficiently. It is a good plan to head swiftly to the far side of the park (**Terrors of the Deep**) when you first arrive and leave the crowds floundering about near the entrance.
The Shamu shows are very popular, so turn up early to get a good seat. (A 'good' seat at a Shamu show, incidentally, depends on your love of water. The first 14 rows get soaked by a playful killer whale dusting up a mini-tidal wave. Watch your camera!)
SeaWorld has similar facilities to WDW for visitors: stroller and wheelchair rental, nappy-changing areas, first aid posts, currency exchange, rentable lockers, kennels, and so on, and everything is similarly well kept, clean, and attractive, though landscaping lacks the Disney sparkle. Smoking is not permitted within the attraction areas. Staff are pleasant and friendly, the tone set by the sign

SEA WORLD

KEY WEST DOLPHIN FEST
An impressive 30–minute show of jumping, diving and splashing provided by dolphins and whales. Funky tropical beach theme with music.

SHAMU STADIUM
The mega-star and relatives cavort in an enormous stadium, where a vast video screen makes life easier for those at the back. Beware of the splash-zone unless you need cooling down.

WILD ARCTIC
A brilliant polar experience. Board a 'jet helicopter' to a remote research station where you will see walruses, beluga whales and, of course, polar bears playing in their sub-zero habitats.

WATERSKI SHOW
A couple of shows a day are held in the Atlantis Bayside Stadium, with stunt skiing and waterski ballet.

PACIFIC POINT RESERVE
The rocky shores here provide a naturalistic setting for the playful California sea lions and seals.

MANATEES: THE LAST GENERATION?
View the Florida manatee from above and below the water in their beautiful lagoon and learn about the fight to beat their extinction.

JOURNEY TO ATLANTIS
This is a water-coaster based on a lost world battle between Hermes and Allura. Combines high-speeds with state-of-the-art special effects.

KRAKEN
Named for an underwater beast kept caged by Poseidon, this is the fastest (65mph), tallest (151–feet) and longest (4,177–feet) roller coaster in Orlando. You go through seven inversions – including a cobra roll, zero-gravity roll and numerous vertical loops and flat spins.

DISCOVERY COVE

Interactive marine adventures are the specialty of SeaWorld's sister park, Discovery Cove. Admission is limited to 1000 guests per day by advance reservation and covers a whole day of water-based activities, plus lunch. Chief thrill is the Dolphin Lagoon, where guests can swim with Atlantic bottlenosed dolphins. There is the Tropical River waterway which meanders past a sandy beach area and an underwater cave to an aviary housing exotic birds from around the world, swimming and snorkelling in the Coral Reef pool, and stingray encounters in the Ray Lagoon. You will have a reserved time for your dolphin swim, but other facilities are unlimited all day. Expensive but fantastic.
(tel: (407) 370–1280 or (877) 4–DISCOVERY)

UNIVERSAL ORLANDO ✓

Universal Orlando is an all-encompassing resort destination that includes the original movie theme park, Universal Studios; the cartoonish fantasy theme park, Islands of Adventure; and the nightclub/restaurant district of City Walk. two luxury hotels – Portofino Bay and the Hard Rock Hotel – have generated an impressive increase in quantity and quality, which makes it hard to justify spending all your holiday time down the road at Disney.
Still in a quandry where to go? If time limits you to visiting one movie theme park (Universal or Disney–MGM), pick Universal Studios – its more energetic, more creative and more fun

overall. Although it had a rocky start, the bumps have long been smoothed out and the rides are in equal; parts exciting, terrifying, exhilarating, sickening and fun.

Practical Details

To see all the attractions at Universal Orlando you need every bit of a long day for each park, especially if it is busy. You have to plan which things to see first, organise yourself to catch the shows at specific times, and constantly try to outwit the queues. Seeing the shows logically, in a way that will illuminate the process of film-making, is therefore unlikely.
There are no trams here, just two massive multilevel car-

Attractions here are definitely live

parks (write down your space number) and a moving walkway to take you to CityWalk. Use the valet parking if you want to get closer, but be prepared to pay for it.

There are several ticket options available for Universal Orlando. Single day, one park admission tickets are available, but the best bet if you plan to do a 'theme park holiday' is an Orlando Flex Ticket. These are available in two forms; Four-park Orlando ticket – up to seven consecutive days of unlimited admission to Universal Studios, Islands of Adventure, SeaWorld Orlando and Wet 'n Wild. Five-park Orlando ticket – up to ten days consecutive admission to the above parks, plus Busch Gardens Tampa Bay.

UNIVERSAL STUDIOS ✓

A movie-orientated theme park grafted onto a working film and television production facility, Universal Studios invites guests to 'ride the movies' on a 444–acre site divided into six themed districts, covering the Deco and palm trees of Hollywood, to Fisherman's Wharf meets New England San Francisco/Amity.

When you first enter the park, have a good look at the free guide and map they give you with your ticket, and at the **Production Schedule** posted by the turnstiles. To make the most of your time, use the Universal Express system: stop at a kiosk near the ride entrance, get a pass stamped with a ride time, then come

back and ride without the wait. Families with young children may need to make several forays to **Woody Woodpecker's KidZone**. Here tots can sing along with the purple dinosaur in **A Day In The Park With Barney**, follow in the footsteps of a cheeky monkey in the **Curious George Goes To Town** water-based interactive play area (bring dry clothes), explore **Fievel's Playland** and take a ride on **Woody Woodpecker's Nuthouse Coaster**. For a well-needed time-out, take a break at the Animal Actors Stage, where trained dogs, chimps and birds show off their skills in an excellent live performance.

The Front Lot

Mostly taken up with practical stuff like lost children and guest relations, though you will find a tempting fudge shop. Do not hang about. From the main entrance, walk straight ahead up the **Plaza of the Stars**.

Production Central

◆◆◆
THE FUNTASTIC WORLD OF HANNA–BARBERA

Take this in right away if queues do not seem too long.
Hanna–Barbera is not some American sit-com heroine you have not caught up with yet, but a composite of the two successful animation cartoonists Bill Hanna and Joe Barbera, creators of such folk heroes as Yogi Bear, the Flintstones, Scooby Doo and the Jetsons. It is a flight-simulated ride involving a bumpy high-speed

chase with Yogi Bear (a poor driver) to rescue the kidnapped Elroy Jetson. The visual effects of colour, speed and depth are astonishing and colossally expensive.

◆◆◆
ALFRED HITCHCOCK: THE ART OF MAKING MOVIES

The presentation is a little confusing in parts, but it is a great show if you know and love those old thrillers. The Master of Suspense himself presides in his inimitably ponderous style. First there is a 3-D version of *The Birds* (and you thought the original film was scary enough –

wait till those gulls are whirling round the auditorium, pecking your eyes out!). The next part of the show is based on the making of *Psycho*, 'the movie that drove thousands to sponge-baths!'. It is introduced on film by a charming and reassuringly normal Anthony Perkins. The audience learns how Hitchcock used 78 separate camera angles to create those few terrifying seconds in the shower scene, still a classic piece of film-making endlessly dissected by movie hounds. After the tension of the pizzicato violins, it is a relief to learn that the nasty dark stuff washing

UNIVERSAL STUDIOS

1. Alfred Hitchcock: The Art of Making Movies

2. An American Tail Theater

3. Animal Actors Stage

4. Amity and Jaws

5. Back to the Future.... The Ride

6. Café La Bamba

7. E. T. Adventure

8. Earthquake–The Big One

9. Ghostbusters

10. Gory, Gruesome & Grotesque Horror Make-up Show

11. Hard Rock Cafe

12. Hollywood Boulevard

13. International Food Bazaar

14. Kongfrontation

15. Louie's Italian Restaurant

16. Mel's Drive-In

17. Murder She Wrote! Mystery Theater

18. New England

19. New York Street Sets

20. Nickelodeon Studios

21. Production Studio Tour

22. San Francisco/ Fisherman's Wharf

23. Screen Test Home Video Adventure

24. Studio Stars Restaurant

25. The Funtastic World of Hanna-Barbera

26. Wild, Wild, Wild West Stunt Show

27. World Expo

down the plug-hole is – chocolate syrup! Ketchup just would not come out dark enough in black and white. Audience volunteers and professional actors lightheartedly recreate the famous stabbing scene, and further film-set and suspense techniques are revealed in the third staging area. Afterwards, you can wander out to the shop and buy some Bates Motel soap or hand-towels for your favourite house-guests.

◆
PRODUCTION TOUR AND NICKELODEON STUDIOS

A large complex of back-lot sets and studios which can be visited, partly on a tram tour. It is mildly interesting if you can hear the bewildering quick-fire commentary, but a lot of it relates to popular US television (especially kid's) shows with which foreign visitors may be unfamiliar, and it goes on far too long. However, it gives some behind-the-scenes insights into the complexity and variety of location filming.

Take in the thrills – and spills – of the Earthquake ride

New York

You will know you have reached the next set by the architecture, a faithful mock-up of those Manhattan sky-scrapers. Within a few hundred square yards you will find Broadway and Greenwich Village, Little Italy and Upper East Side. Here the more egotistical visitor can have a screen test and take home the resulting charismatic video, or be photographed for a magazine cover shot.

◆◆◆
TWISTER...RIDE IT OUT

After the pre-show you will be ushered before a bucolic country scene. It all goes crazy when an ominous funnel cloud appears on the horizon. The tornado takes centre stage and kicks off a catastrophic cacophony of flying cows, lightning strikes and wails from kids. When its over, you will realise that the ride accomplished in minutes what took the movie hours.

KONGFRONTATION

Everyone has to do this ride. King Kong stalks New York, creating predictable mayhem. You, of course, are helplessly caught in his grip; trapped in an aerial tramway car, your life hangs by a thread as you swing over the East River. The great ape weighs six tons and stands four storeys tall, the largest computer-animated model ever constructed. The sound stage for Kongfrontation is one of the most elaborate in the world, with full-scale helicopter models. At the end of the journey, passengers relive their 'terror' on video, filmed while they were in transit (most of them are laughing!).

THE BLUES BROTHERS

A great impromptu (or so it seems) live show brings back Jake and Elwood to perform a selection of their hottest hits. There is some fantastic singing here.

Hollywood Boulevard

The Beverly Hills and Sunset Boulevard sets house cafés and shops selling Hollywood headgear, sunglasses and movie posters.

TERMINATOR 2: 3–D BATTLE ACROSS TIME

An absolutely unmissable, $24–million 3–D adventure scenario that reunites the original *Terminator 2* team in an electrifying combination of new film footage, special effects and live action. Better than a night at the movies, this attraction promises to have you buzzing all day.

THE GORY GRUESOME AND GROTESQUE HORROR MAKE-UP SHOW

If you are a fan of horror movies, this will be like the British Museum. If not, you will still get a kick out of the blending of comedy and creepy special effects.

LUCY: A TRIBUTE

This attraction presents memorabilia from the life and works of that zany redhead, Lucille Ball.

San Francisco/Amity

The large artificial lagoon and its surrounding streets encompass sets of cheerful seasidey architecture, attractive shops and eating places. Just when you thought it was safe to leave the sidewalk, there is that old White Shark , 'Jaws', dangling by the quayside.

EARTHQUAKE – THE BIG ONE

A compelling simulated subway ride through San Francisco when all hell breaks loose, accompanied by an interesting film and demonstration of how these incredibly realistic special effects are achieved.

JAWS

More high-tech special effects as the big fish takes a snap at your excursion boat. A gentle sightseeing cruise with Amity

Boat Tours turns into something altogether snappier with an appearance by that notorious 32–foot mechanical white shark in the corny, but enduringly popular, ride. Have your camera ready!

WILD, WILD, WILD WEST STUNT SHOW

Popular show held several times daily in a stadium at the far side of the complex. Lots of hammy stuff with trick sharpshooting, brawling, explosives, jumping off buildings, abseiling down wires, and so on. The audience is warned not to try these things at home, as they may be quite dangerous!

BEETLEJUICE'S ROCK 'N ROLL GRAVEYARD REVUE

In an amphitheatre off the streets of New york, Beetlejuice's Graveyard Review features classic monsters singing Mowtown songs – great fun.

World Expo Center

Several slick eating places, and some very popular rides, including Universal's *pièce de résistance*:

◆◆◆
BACK TO THE FUTURE

This suffers somewhat from promotional overkill. By the time you get on this ride (after queueing long and hard), you are so determined it is the biggest thing since Ben Hur that the reality is almost bound to disappoint. Yes, it is exciting,

thrilling, technically wizard, using multi-channel surround sound and seven-storey hemispherical screens. But it is only a simulation, and if you have been on a few of these rides you will have an idea what to expect. Nevertheless, theme-parkers, you have to do this one.

◆◆
ET ADVENTURE

Join Steven Spielberg's lovable alien in a new adventure on a star-bound bicycle traversing redwood forests and cities to the Green Planet and its extraordinary magic flowers. Wonderful special effects. It is a nice ride for children of all ages. The queuing system here is good too - well related to the ride and should keep the children occupied for longer than some, however it is quite dark.

◆◆
ANIMAL PLANET LIVE!

Remember that advice about never appearing on screen with children and animals? Here the animals have it all their own way. Find out how these furred and feathered stars are trained, and see them strut their stuff. A good show.

◆◆◆
MEN IN BLACK ALIEN ATTACK

An interactive ride through dark city streets where you fire a laser gun at aliens who pop up in unexpected places. Guests fight it out with the aliens to protect the security of the planet.

ISLANDS OF ADVENTURE ✓

A larger-than-life, primary-coloured cartoon world straight out of the comics (and blockbuster movie Jurassic Park), Islands of Adventure is hailed as the world's most technologically advanced theme park. There is an additional feather in the parks elaborate and distinctly wacky cap, too: it boasts producer/director Steven Spielberg as its creative consultant. Like its sister park, Universal Studios, Islands of Adventure is arranged into themed 'islands' around a central lagoon, known as the Inland Sea. Guests arrive in the souk-like Port of Entry and travel from island to island via boats or footbridges.

Marvel Super Hero Island

Wonderful bold and primary colours transport you straight into a comic strip.

◆◆◆
INCREDIBLE HULK COASTER

This fantastic green roller coaster blasts riders from zero to 40mph in two seconds, with the same thrust as a US Air Force F–16 fighter jet, and follows up with a weightless, zero–G heart-line inversion, seven roll-overs and two plunges into subterranean enclosures.

◆◆
DOCTOR DOOM'S FEARFALL

A rocketing 200–foot trip to the top of the ride's twin towers and back down, both at terrific speeds.

◆◆◆
THE AMAZING ADVENTURES OF SPIDERMAN

A tour of the *Daily Bugle* offices leads into an epic combination of rides, 3–D film action and special effects as the goodies battle the baddies for control of the Statue of Liberty. Unmissable.

◆◆
STORM FORCE

An indoor attraction starring super heroine Storm in a thunderous special effects spectacular that everyone will love.

The studio's San Francisco set

Toon Lagoon

Take a stroll down **Comic Strip Lane** with its giant cartoon cut-outs before tackling the rides. Its not hard to see that this 'island' found its inspiration in the Sunday comics.

POPEYE & BLUTO'S BILGE-RAT BARGES

A white-water adventure raft ride (and guaranteed soaking) that includes a kitschy-horror encounter with an 18–foot–tall octopus. Take your shoes off and put them in the holder – you'll regret it if you don't.

DUDLEY DO-RIGHT'S RIPSAW FALLS

A rip-roaring log flume ride which follows the 1960s Canadian Mountie character on a wet and wild rescue attempt that drops 75–feet below the surface of the water and straight into the TNT shack as he tries to save his beloved Nell.

Jurassic Park

A world transported from the series of films of the same title.

PTERANODON FLYERS

Get a birds eye view of Camp Jurassic while enjoying this aerial ride from beneath the 10–foot wingspan of your carrier.

JURASSIC PARK RIVER ADVENTURE

A raft trip through lush dinosaur habitats harbouring remarkably lifelike robotic creatures. Things go dramatically wrong when the T–Rex get loose and there is only one escape route.....

JURASSIC PARK DISCOVERY CENTRE

An interactive area helps children extract the last scintilla of information about dinosaurs.

Punch-up at the Wild West Show

Scan a dinosaur egg and watch a raptor hatch

TRICERATOPS ENCOUNTER

This enclosure allows guests to get a close look at a 'live' 10–foot–tall 'animatronic' Triceratops undergoing its bi-annual check-up with a Jurassic Park vet.

The Lost Continent

A fantasy lost world combining elements of medieval dungeons–and–dragons sorcery, the Holy Land crusades and Ancient Greece, the Lost Continent's entertainment offerings are equally eclectic.

DUELING DRAGONS

A twin roller coaster featuring Fire Dragon (red) and Ice Dragon (blue), whose fight for power finds the intertwining coasters racing by each other at 60mph, passing within a foot of the other passengers. To make these close calls even closer, a computer weighs the car to ensure near misses.

THE EIGHTH VOYAGE OF SINBAD

The fabled sailor embarks on a stunt show that includes water explosions, fire dives,   ' shipwrecks and pyrotechnical effects, all staged in a shaded 1,700–seat theatre.

POSEIDON'S FURY:ESCAPE FROM THE LOST CITY

Marked by the crumbling ruins

of the sea god's statue, before a chilly walk-through adventure to Atlantis. Visitors pass through a whirling 17,500–gallon water tunnel before witnessing a fiery encounter between Poseidon and Zeus.

Suess Landing

This visually appealing, whimsical 10–acre island is where Dr Suess's much-loved children's books characters are brought to life.

THE CAT IN THE HAT

A trip through the classic Suess tale, with 130 ride effects and 30 animated characters including, naturally, the Cat In The Hat, Thing 1 and Thing 2 who wreak havoc when they come to play.

CARO-SUESS-EL

An elaborate carousel sporting colourful character mounts with state–of–the–art interactive animation features.

ONE FISH TWO FISH RED FISH BLUE FISH

This ride features Seussian-style, two-passenger fish that must be guided along to a special tune to avoid a soaking from 'squirt posts' dotted about the course.

IF I RAN THE ZOO

Kids can let off steam in interactive playland, w Toe Tickle stations al junior guests to tick of giggling Seussi

Universal Studios offers its guests several festivals throughout the year to spice up your day a little further. You will find details of these on the maps you are handed as you enter the park, but some information are given below.

Mardi Gras at Universal Studios takes place between February and April and is a colourful spectacular of bright floats, costumed actors and street entertainers. The parade is definitely a sight to see and from the floats guests are thrown beads to take home with them. There is live music with the parade and on Saturday there are well-known acts playing.

To celebrate the fourth of July Universal Studios presents an explosive and sparkling firework display.

Before leaving the Islands of Adventure make sure you catch the wonderful fireworks over the Inland Sea. One of the best spots to watch these from is the terrace at the

Meticulous detail on a film set

back of the Jurassic Park Discovery Centre. Make sure you place yourself for the display in plenty of time as some of the bridges are closed off for safety reasons, just before and during the fireworks.

CityWalk
Universal's 30–acre shopping, dining and entertainment complex offers something for everyone. Specialty shops run the gamut from fossils, cigars, sportswear and silver jewellery to **Glow!**, a store selling things that, well, glow. There is a **Hard Rock Live Orlando**, a 2,200-capacity performance venue, plus jazz, reggae and Mowtown spots. Or you can chill out Keys-style at **Jimmy Buffett's Margaritaville**. Racing fans can dine out amidst auto memorabilia at the **NASCAR. Café**; **Pat O'Brien's** re-creates the legendary New Orleans watering hole, complete with duelling pianos; and the **Universal Cineplex** has 20 screens showing the latest box-office hits.

CHURCH STREET STATION

Back in the 1970s this old railroad depot was badly run-down and dilapidated, but a visionary proposal to create a glittery entertainment complex has given Orlando's myriad tourists a valid reason to venture downtown. The core of this mini-theme park is its oldest attraction, the turn-of-the-century-style saloon known as **Rosie O'Grady's Good-Time Emporium**. After the success of this, many other night-spots and restaurants were gradually invented in neighbouring buildings, most recently its ambitious three-storey Victorian shopping centre, known as the **Church Street Exchange** (see **Shopping**, page 91). The enclosed street set, perhaps a hundred yards (90m) long, now houses about a dozen separate attractions. One entrance fee (charge after 17.00hrs only) covers admission to the whole street and all the shows, but you do not have to pay to visit the Exchange shops. The Church Street complex is open from 11.00hrs each day, but the shows happen only during the evenings, so most people arrive towards the end of the day. Especially wild nights at Church Street include Halloween and New Year, when the intended street party atmosphere really takes off. One reason for the success of Church Street Station is the care and quality with which the settings of these wacky dancehalls and eating places have been created. Items have been scavenged from all over the world to decorate and furnish the elaborate fun-palaces: a confessional from a French monastery converted into a phone booth, *fin de siècle* brass chandeliers from a Boston bank, etched mirrors from a Glasgow pub. And yes, it is a real steam train out there. The results are certainly eclectic (indiscriminate, even) but they work. The impression as you walk into any of the attractions is of great richness and glitter; everywhere you look there is something to arouse curiosity. It is fun, imaginative, and pretty!

The stylish Cheyenne Saloon

CHURCH STREET STATION

The entertainments at Church Street are ebullient affairs, and generally the complex appeals to young adults, but there is hardly anything you could not take a child to (minimum age in Phineas Phogg's is 21). The shows start at around 19.00hrs, and are timed so you can catch several in an evening. Most of · the restaurants stay open till midnight, a couple of nightspots till 02.00hrs. Any eating or shopping you do in Church Street will be fairly pricey. To get there, take the Anderson Street Exit 38 from Highway I-4 and follow the signs. There are several places to park.
Open: daily 11.00–02.00hrs. Admission charged after 17.00hrs; reduced for under 13s, free for under 3s.

◆◆◆
ROSIE O'GRADY'S GOOD-TIME EMPORIUM
Dixieland jazz, showboat banjos, and girls with good legs clattering Charlestons or can-cans on the bar-tops recreate an ambience somewhere between the Gay 90s and the Roaring 20s in this brassily ornate saloon, reborn from the shabby old Orlando Hotel. 'Rosie', a Red Hot Momma mistress of ceremonies, makes sure everyone's havin' a real good time. Refreshments include deli-style sandwiches and bizarre cocktails. Show-times start at 19.30hrs.

◆◆
CHEYENNE SALOON AND OPERA HOUSE
The Wild West lives on here in a set lovingly created from gold oak lumber (an old Ohio barn), brilliant stained glass, antique guns and the pews from a Catholic church. Heel-kickin', feet-stompin' shows of Country and Western music, and traditional barbecue fare.

◆
LILI MARLENE'S AVIATOR'S PUB AND RESTAURANT
Aviation memorabilia dangles amid a warm glow of pegged timbers and bevelled glass. Food is hearty ribs, steaks and seafood.

◆
APPLE ANNIE'S COURTYARD
Featuring live music (bluegrass and folk) in a quieter mode, where you may have time to look around at some fine antiques. Natural fruit juices and cocktails.

◆
ORCHID GARDEN BALLROOM
A Victorian fantasy of glass, marble and wrought iron, accompanied by popular hits from the 50s onwards.

◆◆
PHINEAS PHOGG'S BALLOON WORKS
Ballooning memorabilia and high-energy music, popular with a youngish in-crowd. **Nickel Beer** nights on Wednesdays involve 'Happy Hour' prices from 17.30–19.00hrs (5¢ for a beer). Minimum age 21.

◆
CRACKERS OYSTER BAR
A good place to try a bowl of seafood chowder or gumbo with a generously sized glass of Californian white. Downstairs is a well-stocked wine cellar.

BUSCH GARDENS ✓

Newborn crocodiles, Busch Gardens

This massive 300-acre (120-ha) theme park of rides and roller coasters also has over 3,000 real animals of 350 different species, and counts as one of the USA's most important zoos. It plays a significant role in breeding and conserving endangered species. If you can take any more 'family entertainment' after Disney, or indeed if you want an antidote to Disney, you might well make the journey over to Tampa. Busch Gardens is a giant 'Out of Africa' safari park. It first opened in 1959, so is an older attraction than anything at Walt Disney World. That soon becomes apparent: things are just not quite as neat and tidy here – the ponds may be a little clogged with weed, the monorail slightly dilapidated. Its rumbustiously authentic fauna are also distinctly more pungent than the antiseptic animations that inhabit the Disney theme parks.

Practical Details

It is about an hour and a quarter's drive from Walt Disney World to Busch Gardens. From Orlando head west on I-4 towards Tampa, then take I-75. From here take Exit 54 (Fowler Ave) and follow the signs. Busch Gardens is at the intersection of Busch Boulevard and 40th Street, eight miles (13km) north-east of downtown Tampa.

There is a lot to see at Busch Gardens including the newest attraction **Gwazi** – Florida's first duelling wooden coaster and the southeasts largest and fastest. You need at least a day to see everything, more if you want to allow time for the water park called **Adventure Island** (separate admission fee and opening times). Plan to arrive as close to opening time as you can. There is a modest parking fee. Take your hat and sun-cream if it is hot: there is a lot of outdoors at Busch Gardens. The usual cameras, strollers, wheelchairs, lost and found offices, and first aid posts are available. The 'house rules' are similar to those in WDW, though here alcohol is more widely available - after all, Anheuser-Busch (the owners) make the stuff! Transport includes a monorail (somewhat

BUSCH GARDENS

less high-tech than Disney's), a quaint steam locomotive, and a cable-car.

Open: daily 09.30–18.00hrs (longer in summer and at holiday times). Not all the shows take place every day. Children under 2 get in free. Remember – this park can be included on an Orlando Flex Ticket along with Universal Orlando and SeaWorld.

Visiting Busch Gardens

The park is divided into eight differently themed 'lands', a rather similar structure to the large Disney theme parks.

MOROCCO

Evident from the Moorish architecture of fancy tiles and castellated walls, this is the first 'land' as you enter from the parking lot. Moroccan crafts and souvenirs are on display, along with dark-eyed snake charmers, a theatre (regular shows of 60s and country music), and the rather unexpected Mystic Sheiks eight-piece brass marching band. The main attraction here, though, is the **Moroccan Palace**, where a spectacular ice-skating show, *Around the World on Ice*, is held four times daily. The acts are excellent and very well rehearsed. Sets flit from Paris to Egypt to South America to Russia, with some lovely costumes. The juggler is particularly watchable, although the contents of his act have no discernible connection with Morocco.

For a quick snack here, try the **Boujad Bakery** (North African pastries). The **Zagora Café**

does burgers, deli sandwiches and breakfasts. There is an ice cream parlour too.

NAIROBI

There are lots of animals here, including crocodiles and alligators (in separate pens – they don't like each other much), reptiles and fish. Rhino Rally, on the east side of Nairobi, is a safari ride through animal habitats including elephants, white rhinos, cape buffalo and zebras. Nairobi is also a place to pick up the jolly little colonial-looking **Trans-Veldt Railroad** train that chugs round the northern outskirts of the park.

CROWN COLONY

Here you can find the rather un-African Budweiser Clydesdale horses who pull ceremonial drays, and **Crown Colony House**, a full-service restaurant with elaborate colonial Victorian decor. It is one of the most comfortable places for a meal in Busch Gardens, with views over the Serengeti Plain.

◆

SERENGETI PLAIN

This 80-acre (32-ha) expanse of flat Florida countryside does not really look too much like African savannah, but the animals help. Giraffes, antelope, gazelles, ostriches and camels lope about on the plains. Rare species like black rhino are being successfully bred here. To see the animals, take the skyride cable car, monorail, or steam locomotive.

◆◆
TIMBUKTU
A fairground in a desert trading post atmosphere. Thrill rides include the sickening **Phoenix** boat swing, the alarming loop-the-loop **Scorpion** roller coaster, and the whirling **Sandstorm**. The **Dolphin Theater** is here (regular dolphin shows), plus **Das Festhaus** where food and entertainment is of the Germanic variety. Also, games, shops and a juice-bar.

◆◆
CONGO
At the northwest corner of the park a few more animals are in evidence among the rides. On **Claw Island** several beautiful Bengal tigers disdainfully regard their audience from a setting of rocks and waterfalls. Things to do here include the **Congo River Rapids** (white-water raft ride) and the **Python** roller-coaster, a yellow serpent that convolutes its passengers through two complete 360-degree spirals. It is fairly alarming, but does not last long. Also here is the new ride called **Kumba**, which exceeds 60mph and includes a diving loop and a camelback, 360-degree spiral.

◆
STANLEYVILLE
This continues the African theme with the **Stanley Falls** (log flume ride) and the **Tanganyika Tidal Wave**, where screaming passengers plummet down a slide into water and completely drench themselves and any bystanders. There is a shopping bazaar and a variety show in the **Stanleyville Theater**.

◆◆◆
EGYPT
Home of **Montu**,the largest inverted roller coaster in the southeast, this area is surrounded by a massive wall that seems to have come from the valley of the Kings. The roller coaster is fast – if you doubt it check out the sign that reads 'If you wear a prosthetic limb, make sure that it is firmly secured'. Here, you will also catch **Akbar's Adventure Tours** – another variation on the simulator ride.

◆
ANHEUSER–BUSCH BREWERY
This is the tall blocky concrete and metallic structure you may have been wondering about at intervals round the park. You can tour it, at your own pace, and learn lots of worthy things about the company, including their commitment to recyling and the fight against alcoholism. Then you can try some of the stuff free at Hospitality House. Close by, for the predilection of children, is Dwarf Village.

Bar-top entertainment

KENNEDY SPACE CENTER

KENNEDY SPACE ✓ CENTER

What's in a name?

John F Kennedy will be for ever linked with the US space programme. It was his determination to set a man on the moon by the end of the 1960s that provided the initial momentum for those many space missions which culminated in the triumphant Apollo moon landing in 1969. When Kennedy was assassinated in 1963, the whole of the Cape Canaveral peninsula was renamed Cape Kennedy in his memory. Ten years later this decision was confusingly rescinded, and the old name was restored. Cape Kennedy no longer exists. Cape Canaveral, an Air Force station where long-range military rockets were tested after World War II, is the historical site of the early NASA (National Aeronautics and Space Administration) space launches. It is a jutting peninsula of low-lying coastal marshlands, separated from the Florida mainland by two meandering rivers enclosing Merritt Island. The Kennedy Space Center, the modern launch-site for the US space programme, is based on the northern part of this island, and is now Florida's third most popular visitor attraction.

Getting There

It is about an hour's drive from Orlando to the east coast, most

A bus demonstrates the rockets' size

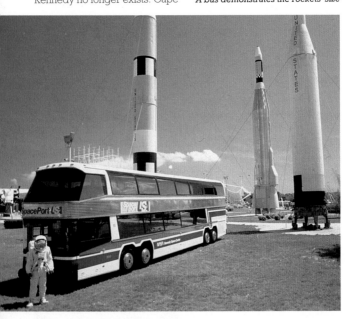

painlessly achieved on the Beeline Expressway which leads past the International Airport. Have some loose change handy for several toll gates. Follow signs for Kennedy Space Center (State Roads 407/405), not Cape Canaveral.

Practical Details

To see everything at the Kennedy Space Center, allow the best part of a day. It is best to arrive early.

Open: 09.00hrs until dusk. There is a lot of hard information (eye-popping statistics, measurements, space facts and figures) to grasp if you are interested, but even if you have only a mild curiosity about the US space programme, the chances are that a visit to the Kennedy Space Center and the military airforce base of Cape Canaveral will enthuse you. Somehow, actually seeing the launch-pad, standing cheek to fuselage with a real Saturn V rocket, makes the great space adventure vivid in a way satellite television never can. Both parking, and admission to **Spaceport USA** (the visitor information centre), are completely free, which must make it one of the best sightseeing bargains in the whole of Florida.

The Spaceport is merely an appetite-whetter for the real stuff of the Kennedy Space Center. To see that, you have to join one of the comfortable, air-conditioned bus tours that leave at frequent intervals to tour the site. There are two bus tours: Red and Blue. Both cost the same; both are worth doing,

with excellent commentaries, boggling statistics and frequent camera stops. As well as the bus tours, there is also a charge for entry to a couple of excellent films (and of course for any food or souvenirs you buy). None of these attractions is at all overpriced, and there are reductions for children aged 3–11.

Despite the futuristic subject matter, however, facilities at the Space Center are not as streamlined or high-tech as at Walt Disney World, nor are there as many staff in attendance to handle crowds. On busy days film shows or tours may get booked up quickly, so as soon as you arrive it is a good idea to reserve a place on whichever bus tours you want, and buy tickets for the IMAX films, *The Dream is Alive*, and *Blue Planet*. Decide whether you are going to eat before or after the tours: they last around two hours, and you will not have a chance to stop for food on the way.

◆◆
MERRITT ISLAND NATIONAL WILDLIFE REFUGE

The road to the Space Center leads over a causeway across the Indian River to Merritt Island, an important nature reserve extraordinarily rich in wildlife (see also page 86). Although it is hard to believe in this high-tech, top-security area, there are more rare and endangered species here than anywhere else on the US mainland. Herons, egrets, ospreys and eagles could well be whirling about with Cape

Canaveral's military jets within easy distance of your car. When rockets periodically roar into orbit with such awe-inspiring force, these blasé creatures scarcely bat an eye. The 7-mile (11km) **Blackpoint Wildlife Drive** through the Merritt Island Refuge enables you to see many different species, and there is a visitor centre. Look out for slow-moving, slow-thinking armadillos on the road. They are often squashed by vehicles.

SPACEPORT USA

By a lagoon near the entrance you will notice the Astronaut's Memorial, a vast 'Space Mirror' honouring the 15 US astronauts who have died in space accidents – a rotating mirror projects their names up to the sky, so that they appear to float among the clouds. Entering the Spaceport is like stumbling into a lunar parking lot. Life-size replicas of modules and skylabs, and some actual space hardware, stand to attention in the open-air **Rocket Garden**, each neatly labelled with a fact-filled information plaque: how big, how fast, how long, how often, and the like. You can clamber aboard the monstrous Ambassador orbiter and see how little elbow-room NASA astronauts have on board a shuttle flight.

Inside the various buildings on the Spaceport you will find cinemas showing space films (including the film, *The Boy from Mars*, a view of life in the 21st century) and many displays and information boards of space

equipment, models, video screens, and so on. A bit of moon rock is proudly displayed.

You could spend any amount of time in here sorting out all those Mercury, Gemini, and Apollo missions. There is some interesting stuff on the Russian Soyuz programme too.

A fairly recent addition, **Satellites and You**, is a 55-minute walk through a simulated space station, with audiovisuals demonstrating how satellites affect life on Earth.

One thing definitely not to miss, however, is the IMAX film *The Dream is Alive*, filmed by astronauts circling the Earth, skilfully narrated by Walter Cronkite, and shown on a screen the size of a five-storey building. The visual effects are absolutely stunning. To recover from this experience, you could head for the **Orbit Cafeteria** and retrieve your hot dog from a revolving carousel.

BLUE BUS TOUR

This takes a more historic perspective, showing visitors the Cape Canaveral base where the earliest space flights were launched.

RED BUS TOUR

This is far more popular, covering the modern launch-site and the administrative and operations buildings. You will learn a bit about the astronauts' training programme, experience an exciting simulated launch (Propellants Pressurised, Forward Arm

The giant IMAX screen at the Galaxy Center is compelling

Retracted, Commit, LIFT OFF), and see a real lunar module – a curious contraption sporting metal instruments at all angles and spider legs draped in yellow tinfoil. On film, watch Neil Armstrong bouncing happily over the moon's surface. Outside again, you head for the massive **Vehicle Assembly Building** (largest roofed structure in the world, capable of holding three and a half dismantled Empire State Buildings). Then gawp at the mammoth **Crawler Transporter**, the largest vehicle in the world, which at its maximum stately pace of 1mph (1.6kph) takes about seven hours to carry rockets the short distance to the launch site. Amazingly, a couple of rare bald eagles nest along this route, presumably regarding

the space-craft as some sort of kindred aerial species. You get a close-up of a vast Saturn V rocket, like the one that carried *Apollo* to the Moon, and finally a glimpse of the launch platform itself, where there just might be a shuttle spacecraft being readied for action. You would have to be very, very cool not to be impressed.

◆◆
SEEING A LAUNCH
If you are seriously interested in the space programme, you might try timing your visit to coincide with an actual launch. Obviously schedules may easily be affected by weather or technical hitches, so it is not worth rearranging your plans too drastically. But if there is a chance, the drill is to head out the night before (stay somewhere in Titusville or Cocoa Beach), get up hideously

early, and prepare for a long wait with countless other space techno-freaks. Ask the information centre at the Spaceport for a handout on where to find the best viewpoints, and so on. (You could, of course, watch a launch more conveniently on TV from any motel room, but that would lack mettle!)

◆
UNITED STATES ASTRONAUT HALL OF FAME

This attraction is under separate management from the Space Center and charges its own admission fees (reductions for 3–12-year-olds). You will spot it before you reach the Space Center, on NASA Parkway (State Road 405) at Titusville. Inside the Hall of Fame, multimedia presentations (video footage and recorded interviews, personal memorabilia, films, models and diagrams) portray the lives and achievements of the first American astronauts, including John Glenn, Alan Shepard, and the ill-fated *Challenger* crew. Lots of hero-worship, but after all, these were heroes. The Hall recently opened **Shuttle to Tomorrow** orbiter; inside the orbiter's cargo bay visitors take a 12-minute space trip through a multi-sensory video presentation.
Open: daily 09.00–17.00 hrs. (tel: 321/269 6100; www.astronauts.org)
In the same building is the **US Space Camp**, where visitors can experience hands-on astronaut training. Children bunk out of school for five-day courses to

become fully fledged space-persons with the one-sixteenth Gravity Chair, the Multi-Axis Simulator and the Space Shuttle Orbiter Simulator. On top of the building is an **Observation Deck**, from where you can see the Spaceport area – and perhaps even see a live space shuttle launch if you are very lucky.

WHAT ELSE TO SEE IN ORLANDO

Some (but not all) of these sights are pretty small beer, a fact not always evident from their admission charges. It is worth planning ahead and being selective about what really interests you, or you could end up frustrated, wasting time and money.

INTERNATIONAL DRIVE AREA

◆
MYSTERY FUN HOUSE
5767 Major Boulevard
Mild frissons of terror with the Egyptian Tomb, the Wizard's 15 Chambers of Surprise, the mirror maze, and the Starbase Omega laser game (additional charge). After that, play with the pinball machines and video games. Mini-golf is available. *Open:* daily 10.00–22.00hrs (midnight in summer).

Restaurants
Among the tacky fast-food chains and diners is a good selection of really superior eating places. **The Peabody Hotel**, 9801 International Drive

(tel: 352 4000) has three good restaurants, all very different, but all pricey: **Dux** is smart, formal and intimate, with one of the highest Triple A accolades in Orlando (cooking a marriage of American and oriental styles); **Capriccio** is in North Italian trattoria style; the **B-Line Diner** is a popular 50s-style café/bar open all day. **Ming Court**, 9188 International Drive (tel: 351 9988) is the classiest

Chinese around this area, with dishes of all the great styles: Mandarin, Szechuan, Hunan and Cantonese. **Bongo's Cuban Café**, at Downtown Disney Westside, has a fun atmosphere, live music and hearty cuban cooking (tel: 828 0999). **Enzo's on the Lake** is very popular with locals and situated beside the picturesque Lake Fairy. Menu features specialties from Rome and

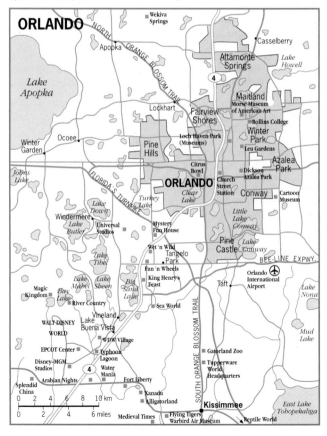

WHAT ELSE TO SEE

Venice (tel: 834 9872) 1130 US 17/92, Longwood.1001).Also serving good Italian food is the **Portobello Yacht Club** at Pleasure Island (tel: 934 8888). For stylish Floribbean cuisine, in a sophisticated dining room on the 28th floor of the downtown Bank of America building, try **Manuel's on the 28th** (tel; 246 6580) at 390 N. Orange Avenue.

LAKE WALES

About an hour's drive south-west of Orlando is a peaceful wooded area of lakes and citrus groves, popular for fishing, camping and boating. Head west on I-4 in the Tampa direction, then take US27 South.

BOK TOWER GARDENS

Three miles (5km) north of Lake Wales. Follow signs along Alt 27 from US27. (Map, pages 16-17.)
The 255-foot (78m) **Singing Tower** of pink and grey marble makes a landmark for miles around. Crowning Florida's highest point (at about 300 feet (91m) above sea level that is not saying much!), it forms the centrepiece of a splendid 128-acre (52-ha) garden of azaleas and other flowering shrubs, which was donated to the American people in 1929 by the Dutch immigrant writer, Edward W. Bok. The tower contains an elaborate carillon of 57 bronze bells which serenade visitors with a great mix of melodies every half-hour (special 45-minute recital at 15.00hrs).
There are no rides or shows or blaring microphones in this

garden: just birdsong and the sound of bells. It is a marvellous antidote to the fevered artificiality of the theme parks, and entrance is relatively cheap by Orlando standards (under–12s free).
Open: daily 08.00–17.00hrs.

◆◆
CYPRESS GARDENS

Off US27 near Winter Haven – follow signs.
(Map, pages 16-17.)
A much larger and more commercialised attraction than Bok Tower Gardens, owned by Disney's great rivals Anheuser–Busch (who also run Sea World and Busch Gardens). It has the distinction of being Orlando's oldest theme park, predating Disney by over 30 years. Created from swampland in 1936, it consists of 223 acres (90 ha) of carefully manicured gardens, shows, restaurants, shops and rides. The **'Mum'** (chrysanthemum) **Festival** every November is as showily spectacular as the gorgeous southern belles who embellish the gardens in their hooped petticoats. Ancillary diversions include performing birds, an eye-catching waterski and microlight show, boat rides through the gardens, a model railroad, antique carousel, Kodak's Island in the Sky (a circular viewing platform raised and lowered periodically by a hydraulic lift), and 8,000 species of plants from 75 countries.
Though gaudy in parts, the gardens are undoubtedly well kept, with lots of botanical interest. Less plant-minded folk

will also have plenty to see and do. Admission charges are quite expensive, so allow time to make the most of everything the attraction offers. (If you visit other Busch attractions, such as Sea World, you can get a discount.) During the shows the atmosphere can be distractingly noisy.
Open: daily 09.30–17.00hrs.

Restaurants
Chalet Suzanne Restaurant and Country Inn (see also **Accommodation**, page 101), between Bok Tower and the Cypress Gardens just off US27 (exit 17A), has an unusual and excellent restaurant. It is well worth booking ahead for lunch or dinner if you are planning a trip out to the Lake Wales area, though the restaurant alone merits the journey. Specialities include Chicken Suzanne, Rum Cream Pie, and the legendary Soup Romaine, which the Apollo astronauts sampled on their moon-landing flight (tel: 941 676 6011, toll-free 800 433 6011).

LAKE COUNTY

FLORIDA CITRUS TOWER
On US27 in Clermont, 45 minutes west of Orlando.
(Map, pages 16-17.)
This is about as high as you can get in Florida without a hot-air balloon. The observation tower surveys the citrus groves, which you can also tour on foot or by tram, and you may sample the produce in candied or marmalade form. The surrounding complex includes many other attractions. Under-9s go free. *Open:* daily

The Cypress Gardens are Orlando's oldest theme park

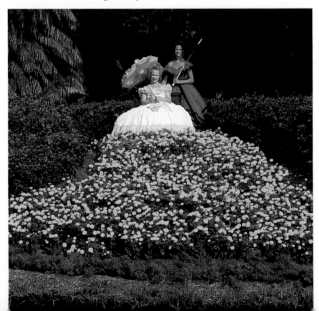

08.00–18.00hrs (restaurant
07.00–21.00hrs). Nearby on
US27 North is the **Lakeridge
Winery** – free daily tours, plus
the chance to taste some of
Florida's local offerings.

NORTHERN ORLANDO
As you leave Orlando city on I-
4 heading north-east towards
Daytona, you pass the museum
park of **Loch Haven**, a smart
residential suburb called
Winter Park, and the historic
riverside community of
Sanford. Further out are the
rural resorts of **Wekiva
Springs** and old Floridian
villages like **Mount Dora** and
Apopka, popular with
campers, walkers and lovers of
the Great Outdoors. Also in this
direction is the spiritualist
camp of **Cassadaga**.

LOCH HAVEN PARK
*Take Exit 43 off I-4 (Princeton
Street), then head a mile east*
A lakeview landscaped park
(picnics, kite-flyers, and so
on). Three small museums
and some pleasant gardens
are worth a glance if
you're passing, though not a
special detour.

Orange County Historical
Museum
Somewhat jumbled exhibits on
Orange County's early
development, at 812 East
Rollins Street.
Open: Monday to Saturday
09.00–17.00hrs; Sunday
12.00–17.00hrs.
At the rear is Orlando's oldest
standing fire station, dating from
1926. Early fire-fighting

vehicles and equipment,
photographs and murals.
Open: Monday to Saturday
09.00–17.00hrs; Sunday
12.00–17.00hrs.

Orlando Museum of Art
Undergoing renovation, this
museum on 2416 North Mills
Avenue contains a fine
collection of pre-Columbian
art from South America, 19th-
and 20th-century American
art, African artefacts, and
periodically changing
exhibitions. Admission is
inexpensive.
Open: Tuesday to Saturday
09.00–17.00hrs; Sunday
12.00–17.00hrs. *Closed:*
Monday.

Orlando Science Center
777 E. Princeton Street
The centre displays
educational exhibits for
children, including plenty to
touch and experiment with. The
John Young Planetarium hosts
daily starshows and cosmic
concerts at weekends
(additional charge).
Open: Tuesday to Thursday
(and school holiday Mondays)
09.00–17.00hrs; Friday and
Saturday 09.00–21.00hrs;
Sunday 12.00–17.00hrs.

Leu Gardens
1730 N. Forest Ave
Fifty seven acres of winding
paths through camellias,
azaleas, rose gardens,
woodland and palms. The
floral clock is one focal point;
so too is **Leu House Museum**
(1730 North Forest Avenue),
a turn of the century
Floridian farmhouse.
Museum open: Tuesday to

A Tiffany window, Morse Museum

Saturday 10.00–16.00hrs;
Sunday and Monday
13.00–16.00hrs. *Grounds open*
daily, 09.00–17.00hrs.
Restaurants
If you are downtown, head for
**Townsend's Fish House and
Tavern** (same management as
the **Apopka Townsend's**)
where a yuppy crowd gathers
for snacky things to accompany
a good range of wines by the
glass, 35 West Michigan Street
(tel: 422 5560). A little further
north, **Café on the Park** serves
steak, shellfish and Sunday
brunch overlooking sparkling
Lake Eola, 151 East Washington
Street (tel: 841 3220).

WINTER PARK
This posh district, formerly a *fin
de siècle* winter resort for the
wealthy, has a lovely setting on
a string of lakes, now surrounded
by millionaire mansions.
Characterised by smart
'European-style' shops, art
galleries, up-market restaurants,
chic bars and one of Orlando's
most elegant hotels, Winter Park
is a pleasant and relaxing place

to visit, or even to base yourself
for a few days. It has a theatre
and two small art museums (the
Morse Museum – see below –
and the **Cornell Fine Arts
Museum**, in Rollins College).

Morse Museum of American Art
445 Park Avenue North
Despite the attempts of the
curator to widen the appeal of
this charming little museum, the
prize contents are undoubtedly
the glorious Tiffany mosaic
windows and art nouveau glass.
Much of this was rescued from
Laurelton Hall, Tiffany's Long
Island home, after a disastrous
fire. Iridescent blue vases are
among the most eye-catching
pieces (tel; 645 5311).
Open: Tuesday to Saturday
09.30–16.00hrs; Sunday
13.00–16.00hrs.
Closed: Monday.

Park Avenue
A tempting street for luxury,
novelty or book shopping (see
page 91), with a peaceful park
of fountains and palms. The

WHAT ELSE TO SEE

Park Plaza Hotel and its excellent restaurant are here (see below). Most shops open from 10.00hrs.

Scenic Boat Tour

An hour-long cruise through lakes and canals, with wildlife (ospreys and snakebirds), luxury houses and the Mediterranean-style **Rollins College** campus. Daily tours from Osceola lakeshore, every hour from 10.00 to 16.30hrs (tel: 644 4056).

Restaurants

Winter Park has a classier collection of restaurants and bars than just about anywhere else in Orlando, so try to eat here if you visit. One of the best and most famous eating places is the restaurant of the Park Plaza Hotel, the **Park Plaza Gardens**, 319 Park Avenue South (tel: 645 2475). In a conservatory setting of lush vegetation you can enjoy classic continental cooking. They are good on seafood, and Sunday brunch (11.00–15.00hrs) is something of an institution. Vying with it for the

*The elegant **Grand Romance**, on the river at Sanford*

top end of the market is the beautifully decorated **La Belle Verrière**, full of gorgeous Tiffany stained glass. Classic French, with local ingredients like catfish; 142 Park Avenue South (tel: 645 3377).

Pebbles is a casual restaurant, which serves creatively interpreted Italian–American fare – good pasta dishes with a wide range of accompaniments such as duck and wild mushrooms – and a fine selection of wines; 2516 Aloma Avenue (tel: 678 7001). For sheer fun, **Bubbalou's Bodacious BBQ** dishes up hot fast food on rustic picnic tables beneath dangling baseball caps, 1471 Lee Road (tel: 628 1212).

SANFORD

(Map, pages 16-17.)
This little community played an interesting role in the local citrus industry, and still retains a few buildings that in Florida count as historic. Its river and

lakeshore location now make it a tourist centre, particularly for regattas and cruises. If you need a base up here, there is a handily placed **Holiday Inn** right on the waterfront. Take Exit 51 from I-4, then head five lights east into Sanford.

Big Tree Park
General Hutchinson Parkway, Longwood
Close to Sanford, the Big Tree Park is home to 'The Senator', a 3,500-year-old bald cypress tree, one of the oldest and, at 138-foot tall, largest trees in America. The park is open daily with free admission.

Rivership *Grand Romance*
433 North Palmetto Avenue, by the marina
Leisurely dining cruises down the St John's River on this nostalgic-looking sidewheeler paddle steamer (built in 1989!). Daily and evening sailings with food and music, dancing Friday and Saturday evenings (tel: 321 5091, toll free 800-423 7401). Cruises last three or four hours.

Restaurants
For a lunchtime snack, you could try **Christo's** at 107 West 1st Street (tel: 322 3443), a Greek-deli diner with everything from snacks to full meals: filling soups, spinach in filo pastry, and so on.

◆
CASSADAGA
Take Exit 54 from I-4, then county road 4139. (Map, pages 16–17.)
Definitely different, an excursion to the Spiritualist Camp is popular on Sundays. A community of varied mediums has settled in a wooded clearing. Visitors are welcome to turn up any day for psychic readings of palms, Tarot cards, crystal balls, and spiritual counselling. Rates start from about $20. You can either wander round the houses looking at the signboards and beating on doors, or head for the bookshop for information on who is in session that day.

◆
SILVER SPRINGS
Exit 69 off I-75, one mile (1.6km) east of Ocala on SR40. (Map, pages 16–17.)
Popular with outdoor enthusiasts, the area offers jungle cruises, trips in glass-bottomed boats, Jeep safaris, and crystal-clear springs that discharge around 500 million gallons (2,275 million litres) of water a day. Animals from six continents, petting zoo, animal shows, dinosaur exhibits, water park, picnic sites, camping, etc. *Open:* daily, 10.00–17.00hrs (extended hours in summer and holidays).

Restaurants
If you are heading this far north, catch a meal at one of the local resorts. Several are worth a special excursion. **Jordan's Grove** at 1300 South Orlando Avenue, Maitland (tel: 628 0020, not Mondays) is a fine old house with ambitious game, veal, and lamb dishes as well as many simpler choices, with interesting American wines. Nearby, at 9495 South US Highway 17–92 (tel: 831 0442) the **Chesapeake Crab House** serves, crab!

WHAT ELSE TO SEE

Maison & Jardin, the 'Mason Jar', is another converted mansion with white arches and lovely garden views. International dishes are served with panache; 430 South Wymore Road, Altamonte Springs (tel: 862 4410).

In Apopka village, at 604 East Main Street, **Historic Townsend's Plantation**, a splendid Victorian mansion, has satisfying southern specialities such as coconut-fried shrimp, Cajun alligator tail and, of course, fried chicken (tel: 880 1313).

SOUTHERN ORLANDO

Heading east from Walt Disney World on Highway 192 takes you through the Kissimmee belt of unlovely commercial development, but there are several minor attractions in this direction, including many shopping malls and dinner-show venues (see **Shopping** and **Nightlife**).

◆

XANADU – HOME OF THE FUTURE

4800 Irlo Bronson Memorial Highway
Tomorrow's domestic world – 15 rooms of sculptured walls and computer-controlled gadgetry.
Open: 10.00–22.00hrs.

◆

WORLD OF ORCHIDS

2501N Old Lake Wilson Road, Kissimmee
Recently opened, it holds the world's largest permanent exhibition of exotic and rare orchids with over 2,000 flowers in bloom all year in its indoor conservatory. On US route 192 on State Road 545. A worldwide shipping service and sales catalogues are also provided. (tel; 396 1817).

SPLENDID CHINA

3000 Splendid China Boulevard, Kissimmee (State Road 192)
This Chinese-themed journey takes visitors on a '10,000 mile trip through 5,000 years of Chinese history and culture' in a 76-acre park setting. There are over 60 miniaturised replicas of China's historic landmarks, including the **Great Wall**, **Forbidden City** and **Terracotta Warriors**. It also features live Chinese-themed entertainment, with jugglers, acrobats, storytellers and demonstrations of martial arts. (tel: 800 244 6226).

GATORLAND

14501 South Orange Blossom Trail (US441)
Probably not for animal lovers, despite the strenuous emphasis on 'conservation, education and research'. Alligators that once plagued the swampy cattle ranches of Florida are now farmed for their mottled skins and, as a by-product, their meat. Here you can see lots of alligators of all sizes: hatchlings to leathery 80-year olds. Even cuddle one if you fancy it (jaws carefully taped!). 'Gator-wrestlin' demonstrations and 'Gator Jumparoo' shows are held several times a day by ex-'crackers' (Floridian cow-

hands). This is not particularly cruel, just intensely irritating to the somnolent reptiles who would rather bask unmolested and give their marble-sized brains a rest. A swamp walk gives you a less artificial view of the creatures, and an observation tower over part of the farm gives a good idea of an alligator's natural habitat, in other words, a picture of central Florida before the theme parks arrived. Then you get to eat an alligator (it's better than the other way round), or you can buy alligator products (cowboy boots are very expensive; tins of gator chowder less so). *Open:* daily, 09.00–18.00hrs (longer in school holidays and peak season) (tel: 800 393 JAWS)

◆

TUPPERWARE WORLD HEADQUARTERS
Next to Gatorland on US441 South
Self-guided tours every half-hour through the plush offices, with a short film on the manufacturing process, and displays of the full range of Tupperware products. You can, of course, order it here, but there is no high-pressure sales talk. There is also a collection of food containers from the Egyptians to the present day. Tours are free.
Open: weekdays 09.00–16.00hrs.

◆

REPTILE WORLD SERPENTARIUM
Four miles (6.5km) east of St Cloud on US192
Not for snake phobics. Self-guided tours take you past 60

reptilian species from Florida and the rest of the world. Watch the venom being extracted for biomedical research at 11.00, 14.00 and 17.00hrs.
Open: Tuesday to Sunday 09.00–17.30hrs. *Closed:* Monday and September.

Restaurants
Red Lobster at 5690 W. Irlo Bronson Memorial Highway (tel: 396 6997), you'll find good quality seafood and service. **Le Coq au Vin** is, naturally, French, friendly and highly competent (rainbow trout, Long Island duck, frog's legs, goat's cheese), 4800 South Orange Avenue (tel: 851 6980). For something different, try **Gain's German Restaurant** at 5731 S. Orange Blossom Trail East Colonial Drive (tel: 438 8997).

WATER PARKS
Nicer from the setting and landscaping point of view are unquestionably WDW's Typhoon Lagoon and River Country (see pages 49). If adrenalin is what counts, you may prefer those below. Note that although lifeguards are present at all times, back and neck injuries are not unknown. Observe all warning notices, and instructions carefully.

WATER MANIA
6073 West Irlo Bronson Memorial Highway (US192)
A 38-acre site of chutes and flumes, surf lagoons, wooded picnic grounds, mini-golf courses, and Anaconda raft rides. There is also an 8,100-sq-foot (752-sq-metre) maze.

WHAT ELSE TO SEE

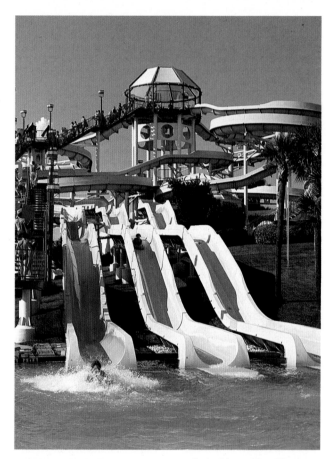

Splash out at Wet'n Wild

Open: March–September, daily 10.00–17.00hrs; October, Wed–Sat only 10.00–17.00hrs.

◆◆
WET'N WILD
6200 International Drive (Exit 30A South off I-4)
Unmistakably artificial tubes and slides squirm into huge pools, at this exciting 25-acre (10-ha) water park. Look out for the alarming **Black Hole** – a headlong Cresta Run and **Bomb Bay** a free-fall down a 76-ft slide.
Open: daily but variably depending on season; 09.00–21.00hrs max; 10.00–17.00hrs min. Discount admission operates late in day; under-3s go free all day.

Peace and Quiet

Countryside and Wildlife around Orlando by Paul Sterry

Few holiday destinations can rival Orlando for the sheer scale of tourist attractions, and Walt Disney World offers more than enough to satisfy many of those who visit central Florida. However, there is another side to Orlando, and those prepared to step aside from the familiar routes will discover that the surrounding area has superb natural locations which are rich in wildlife.

Wekiva Springs State Park

This wooded park lies 18 miles (29km) northwest of Orlando and is an ideal spot for combining peace and quiet with birdwatching. Take route US441 from Orlando as far as Apopka, and then head west on route 436. The entrance is signposted off to the left. Park in designated areas and walk the trails and paths through the open pine woodland looking for birds such as bobwhite quails, small gamebirds that are usually seen in parties of half a dozen or so. You should also keep a sharp lookout for red-shouldered hawks, woodpeckers and warblers.

Kelly County Park

This park is contiguous with Wekiva Springs State Park. Take US441 as far as Apopka and then head north on route 435 until you see the park entrance on your right. Look for woodland birds and mammals such as squirrels in the pine woodland.

Audubon House

Audubon House, in Maitland, is the headquarters of the Florida Audubon Society, the State's leading bird study and

The green heron is a year-round resident of Florida

PEACE AND QUIET

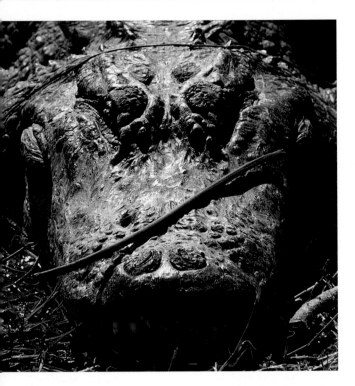

American alligator

conservation organisation.
Information about birdwatching
in the Orlando district can be
obtained here. There is also a
bird of prey care and
rehabilitation centre. The house
is on Lake Avenue (route 438A).

Moss County Park

An ideal spot for birdwatching,
this park is 20 miles south of
Orlando and can be reached by
turning south off the Beeline
Expressway (route 528) on to
route 15 and driving for about 3
miles (5km). Look for woodland
birds and sandhill cranes in the
grassy wetlands and open pine
forest. There are trails within
the park itself.

Lake Monroe

Lake Monroe lies near Sanford,
to the north of Orlando. To
reach it take I-4 north from the
city and turn off on route 17,
heading south for a couple of
miles. The shores of the lake
can be seen from the road –
look for ducks, egrets and
herons, especially during the
winter months. Adjacent to Lake
Monroe is the **Central Florida
Zoological Park**, on route 17. In
addition to the captive animals
and birds, native wild birds can

be found in abundance in and around the swampy areas. If you drive north on route 17 from Lake Monroe, crossing I-4, you will see **Blue Springs State Recreation Area** signposted to the right. It is good for woodland and water birds as well as the occasional manatee. Further north still on route 17 is **Lake Woodruff National Wildlife Refuge** (turn off at Deleon Springs). This is a superb area for water birds.

Lake Jessup

Lake Jessup lies north of Orlando, close to Sanford. Head north on route 17 from the city and take route 46 east just before you reach Sanford. The

American Alligators

Once persecuted for their skin and because they are perceived as a threat to man, alligators have staged something of a comeback in recent years. They can now be found in many of Florida's waterways and are an interesting, if somewhat awesome feature of the native wildlife. Alligators lay their eggs in sandy banks but spend much of their time in water. They feed mainly on fish but will also take water birds if the opportunity arises. It is not uncommon to see alligators exceeding 10 feet (3m) in length these days – these are probably more than 20 years old.

Vultures

Almost anywhere you drive in central Florida, you are likely to see vultures. They often circle overhead and will even visit roadsides in search of animal road casualties. Two species are found in Florida. The black vulture is, as its name suggests, largely black and in flight has broad wings and a comparatively short tail. The turkey vulture also has black plumage but the head is bald and red in colour. In flight, turkey vultures have long wings with a trailing paler margin and a relatively long tail. Sometimes vultures can be seen circling over towns and cities – even Orlando. Although they are bold when it comes to feeding, they are shy birds when nesting, and the nests themselves are seldom seen.

road passes close to the northern margin of the lake where the marshy habitat is home to birds such as egrets, herons, rails and ducks – look from the bridge. Nearby **Mullet Lake Park** can be reached if you continue east on route 46 for a short while and turn left into Osceola Road. Woodland birds and insect life abound in this tropical oak 'hammock' and the marshes and fields are also full of birds.

Lake Tohopekaliga

This extensive lake lies to the south of Orlando, not far from Kissimmee. From Kissimmee, head south on route 17 and then turn off on route 531. At Overstreet Road, turn left towards the lake shore. Look for egrets, herons, bald eagles, ducks and pelicans.

PEACE AND QUIET

Merritt Island National Wildlife Refuge

On a trip to the John F Kennedy Space Center and Cape Canaveral, visitors who are interested in wildlife should not miss the Merritt Island National Wildlife Refuge. This vast area of lagoons, freshwater and brackish marshes and mangroves – more than 140,000 acres in all – offers some of the best birdwatching in Florida. The coastal scenery, although flat, provides a pleasant setting for anyone intent on a seaside stroll.

To reach the refuge, take route 402 from Titusville across to Merritt Island. Almost anywhere can be good for wildlife but the following spots may be particularly productive.
Having crossed to Merritt Island, ignore the right fork (Beach Road) and continue to the **Blackpoint Wildlife Drive**, a loop road where you can use

Snowy egret

Snowy Egret

Even the smallest ponds, ditches or marshes in central Florida are likely to host birds such as herons and egrets, which thrive on the abundant frogs and fishes. Among the most attractive and distinctive of these is the snowy egret, an aptly named bird with pure white plumage. In the breeding season it develops long plumes on its head, and at all times it has black legs with contrasting yellow toes and shins. Snowy egrets are patient fishers, wading slowly through the shallows until their prey comes within reach. In common with many of Florida's other birds, they are curiously indifferent to people, and can often be watched at extremely close range without being disturbed.

your car as a hide. Then retrace your tracks and follow Beach Road to the **Canaveral National Seashore** where you can look for waders, gulls and terns. Retrace your route again along Beach Road and follow signs to the Visitor Center for information about the refuge. As an alternative, you may wish to visit the nearby **Ulumay Wildlife Refuge**. From Cocoa take route 520 off US route 1 and cross the bridge on to Merritt Island. Turn north towards Sykes Creek Park and stop at the refuge. This is a superb area for herons, egrets, ibises, waders, terns and warblers, and a nature trail affords superb views of the area.

Practical

This section (with the yellow band) includes food, drink, shopping, accommodation, nightlife, tight budget, special events etc.

FOOD AND DRINK

Say 'Florida' to most people and the first thing that springs to mind is – oranges. About 25 per cent of the world's crop is produced here, and about 95 per cent of the total production of concentrated orange juice. Citrus fruits are stacked up in huge outlets by the roadside for passers-by. Try tangelos (a juicy hybrid), pineapple oranges, pink grapefruit, and Persian limes. Citrus juice is always available at breakfast (though little seems freshly squeezed), and you can also buy citrus jams, marmalades, candy, even citrus wine at roadside factory outlets. Florida also grows other types of fruit and vegetables, notably kumquats, strawberries and sweet corn. Once a great cattle-rearing state, cattle are still important and prime rib steak still features on many a Floridian menu.
Seafood, though, is its main gastronomic staple. Even in central Florida you can find excellent fish restaurants. Clams, rock shrimp (langostino), lobster, crawfish,

pompano and scamp (flaky white fish), mullet, oysters, scallops and stone crabs are common specialities. Fresh palm hearts are a local delicacy.
The range of food available in Orlando is less interesting than the ethnic variety and number of establishments suggests. Much of its cuisine is geared to the unadventurous palates of children, and tends to be bland and inoffensive rather than challenging. So fried chicken, steaks six ways, and ubiquitous pizzas, pastas and burgers are much in evidence. Within the theme parks, the sheer pressure of visitor numbers dictates homogenised mass catering and economies of scale rather than individually prepared dishes. Speed and convenience compensate to some extent. Even though you may have to search a little to find exceptional food in Orlando, you will rarely get a bad meal; standards of hygiene are high, service generally pleasant and efficient, and portions invariably generous. Florida's home-grown cuisine (now rediscovered for the

FOOD AND DRINK

tourism industry) is called 'cracker' cooking, and includes specialities like fried catfish, 'hush puppies' (deep-fried corn meal dough) and, what seems most outlandish of all, alligator meat ('gator tails' or nuggets), which tastes very like salty chicken. However, these homespun curiosities constitute only a tiny fraction of the vast range of ethnic and international food on offer inside and outside the theme parks. Caribbean and Cajun (Louisianian) influences are strong, particularly in gumbo (okra stew), conch chowder and many other Cajun or Creole dishes. Spanish/Mexican/Cuban flavours are imported by Florida's many Latin settlers: black-bean soup, paella, piccadillo, tacos, enchiladas, guacamole. Speciality Asian restaurants abound – Thai, Japanese, Chinese, Indian – plus of course European: Italian, Greek, French, even British. Jewish food bows in with Reubens on rye, cream cheese and lox, chicken livers and pastrami. For the health-conscious, vegetarian, organic or cholesterol-free food makes tiny inroads in the otherwise calorific and fat-laden diet that still prevails in America. Speciality desserts include Key Lime Pie and strawberry shortcake.

Eating hours blur into a steady all-day munch in Orlando. From early in the morning until late at night (all night long if you know where to look) it is possible to find just about anything you like to eat and drink. Remember, though, that you are not allowed to take food or drinks on any of the rides or attractions at WDW. Rules on alcohol are also strict: the legal age for drinking in Florida is 21, and no minors may sit or stand near a bar. No alcohol is allowed within the Magic Kingdom, but other WDW restaurants do serve it. A certain amount of wine is made in Florida but, although quite good for the most part, it does not compare favourably with Californian. Do not bother paying the expensive mark-up for imported European wines while you are there.

Breakfast

A huge range of muffins, bagels, waffles, pancakes, grits (boiled ground corn) and cinnamon toast add ballast to any sort of eggs, fruit, and yoghourt. 'Biscuits and gravy' is a strange but certainly not unpleasant concoction of savoury dough and a white sauce flavoured with sausage. Breakfast is washed down with orange juice, of course, and copious but sometimes watery coffee (you can generally have several refills).

The 'diner' or cafeteria-style restaurants often have very good inclusive deals for breakfast (often better value than hotels, or the theme park restaurants), and if you are theme-parking, it is worth stoking up early for a long hard day. If you have children to amuse, though, they will probably enjoy at least one 'character' breakfast, with Mickey and pals. On Sundays 'brunch' is a spectacular

Broiled Florida grapefruit

mid-morning banquet at
several large hotels including
Park Plaza in Winter Park, and
WDW's Contemporary Resort
and Polynesian Resort.

Lunch

Often cheaper (relatively) than
dinner, so if you want a good
meal, having it at midday may
save you a few dollars. On the
other hand, if sightseeing is
your main object, spending too
much time queueing and sitting
in restaurants may not be a
sensible use of your day.
'Grazing' (that is, munching
snacks at intervals) may be a
better way to satisfy your
appetite. If you do want to sit
down at lunchtime, make a
reservation well ahead for any
of the popular WDW
restaurants, and try to hit
them either early (before noon)
or late (after 14.30hrs) to
avoid the main rush.
Alternatively, head for a resort
hotel, or one of the less
crowded Village restaurants.

Dinner

If you can eat early, before
18.00hrs, some restaurants give
you a discount. There is also
'Happy Hour' to consider in
many cocktail bars (see **Tight
Budget** section, page 109).
Dress codes are normally fairly
relaxed (ties rarely required
except in the very smartest
restaurants), but the air-
conditioning can be quite chilly,
so an extra layer may be useful.
Florida's summer climate
makes eating out of doors an
attractive option, but after dark
remember the insect repellent.

Restaurant Chains

In Orlando's tourist areas you
will find all the well-known
franchised names: Pizza Hut,
McDonalds, Wendys, Burger
King, Kentucky Fried Chicken,
International House of
Pancakes, Baskin Robbins, Taco
Bell. Chains worth looking out
for include Dennys or
Morrison's Cafeteria (good-
value family diners), Red
Lobster (seafood), Bennigan's
(international snacks and
steaks), Pizzeria Uno (guess
what!) and Olive Garden (for
reliable, mid-priced Italian
food). There are any number of
steakhouses: Charley's Steak
House, Barney's Steak and
Seafood, Cattle Ranch, and
Freddie's Steak and Seafood
are some of the best known.

SHOPPING

Retailing is an art form in the USA, and central Florida is a shopoholic's dream. Shops in Orlando are not mundane, practical places of commerce: they are sightseeing attractions in themselves, to some extent filling the gap left by the paucity of cultural or historic interest found in most tourist cities. Besides literally hundreds of shops devoted to the merchandising of Disney souvenirs in and around Walt Disney World, you will see countless shopping malls, markets and discount factory outlets blazoned everywhere in Orlando. Inevitably, a lot of the stuff on sale is rubbish, but never mind. You can have plenty of fun looking at it, and you may just find a real bargain. In the land of the credit card, choosing purchases may be a lot easier than paying for them. You should remember that 6 per cent sales tax is added to the marked prices (except for food bought in a grocery store).

Disney Shopping

If you have children with you it is unlikely that you will escape from Orlando without a few mementos of Mickey. First choice for kids is obviously a set of those famous ears. All over WDW, in hotels, in the theme parks, and in shopping complexes, images of the Mouse and his friends are endlessly replicated in a thousand and one guises – on T-shirts and baseball hats, pens, mugs, watches, and things you have never even thought of. If some of these souvenirs seem pretty tasteless, just wait till you get outside Walt Disney World. A word of warning on Disney shops, however. The range and scale of the eye-catching merchandise within the theme parks may distract you unduly from what will certainly be a gruelling schedule. If you spend too long browsing through the shops, you may miss out on what you really came to do, which is ride those rides. So ration yourself. If you are determined to shop, however, it is easier to do so in the mornings, before queues build. Dump any bulky purchases in the lockers by Guest Relations. There are lots of shops to visit outside the parks, so it is easy to look for souvenirs without lopping time off those rather expensive hours you spend within the turnstiles.

An excellent place to shop without paying entrance fees is **Downtown Disney**, near Lake Buena Vista and the Typhoon Lagoon. This attractive complex houses well over a dozen boutiques selling high-quality souvenirs (*Open:* 10.00–22.00hrs). **Mickey's Character Shop** has the largest range of 'Disneyana' in the world. Toys depicting Disney characters and Muppets in every possible size and shape cram the shelves. Other shops specialise in glass and ceramics, jewellery, candles, or houseware. The imaginative range of stationery at Personal Message is particularly appealing. Nicely designed ink stamps make portable if not inexpensive presents. During the day (10.00–19.00hrs) the nearby shops on Pleasure Island can be visited free of charge. Try Suspended Animation for posters and lithographs, or YesterEars for nostalgia Disney. At Lake Buena Vista, opposite the Hotel Plaza is another Disney-owned shopping centre called the **Crossroads**. Here you will find more practical outlets, including a 24-hour supermarket, a pharmacy, a bank and a post office.

Shopping 'Villages'

Several complexes rival the Disney Marketplace as tourist attractions, offering restaurants and entertainment, as well as shops – in fact, functioning more or less as miniature theme parks in their own right.
Church Street Station is one of the most widely publicised of the shopping 'villages' (see also main entry, page 63, and **Nightlife**, page 102). Most of the shops are in the Exchange, a recently opened attraction with over 60 speciality shops and stalls in a glittering three-storey Victorian-style building. The shops stay open from 11.00–23.00hrs every day, plus a market (Monday–Saturday 10.00–21.00 hrs, Sunday 12.00–18.00hrs) and, unlike the other attractions within the complex, entrance to the Exchange is free. Most people visit during the evenings when the shows are on. Here the emphasis is firmly on fun shopping: magic T-shirts that change colour as you wear them, cheerfully blatant 'smellalike' fragrances, and zirconium 'diamonds'.
Park Avenue, in the smart North Orlando residential district of Winter Park, is one of the classiest places to shop. You will find names familiar in Europe among the shopfronts – Laura Ashley, Crabtree & Evelyn, Benetton. Antiques, smart bedlinen, rugs, posh toys and clothes for children, gourmet delicacies and elegant accessories are among the sophisticated

Shop with the 'stars' on Disney-MGM Studios' evocative Hollywood Boulevard

SHOPPING

offerings. Needless to say, you will need a hefty credit limit to purchase them. Most shops open at 10.00hrs.

Mercado Mediterranean Village is a Spanish-style complex on International Drive, containing over 60 shops of clothes, jewellery and ethnic crafts (Chinese pottery, Toledan daggers), with a bit of street entertainment to keep visitors amused. Shops open 10.00–22.00hrs.

Old Town, Kissimmee, on Highway 192, is a re-creation (hard to imagine in today's Orlando) of Old Florida, where over 70 shops sell a plethora of keepsakes in a setting of brick-paved streets and turn of the century architecture, plus antique carousel and ferris wheel. *Open:* daily 10.00– 23.00hrs.

Mickey gets everywhere

Shopping Malls, Factory Outlets and Flea Markets

The dividing line is fairly thin between the first two, but a mall is a bit posher. The big ones are **Florida Mall** on Sand Lake Road, **Colonial Plaza Mall** on East Colonial Drive, and **Altamonte Mall** north of Orlando. Some of these huge, charmless complexes contain upwards of 175 shops, including famous department stores like Sears, Maison Blanche and JC Penney. Factory outlets claim to give discounts of up to 75 per cent, and amid a great deal of tat you can find some good buys if you can put up with the down-market atmosphere. There are several such outlets on or near **International Drive**. Luggage, cutlery, clothes, shoes, even party stationery, denim and sports equipment can be bought. One of the biggest conglomerations is the **Belz Factory Outlet Mall**, situated in the International Drive resort area, where nearly 150 discount stores can be visited. *Open:* Monday–Saturday 10.00– 21.00hrs; Sunday 10.00– 18.00hrs.

Another large one is the **Quality Outlet Center**. The **Dansk Factory Outlet** is widely advertised, selling well-designed Danish cookware and glass at considerable discounts. North American visitors flock to these malls and load up the car; obviously tourists from overseas have limited space in their suitcases.

Flea markets are held, usually at weekends, in several places around Orlando. There is a large one in Kissimmee, but the biggest is **Flea World** near Sanford. Hundreds of small booths sell anything and everything, and little enough you would want to buy. *Open:* Friday–Sunday 08.00–17.00hrs.

ACCOMMODATION

'Fridge and Micro. Twin Queen Beds. God is Love.' Just a sample of many motel signs whose flickering neon may temporarily distract you on the highways around Orlando. Hundreds of hotels (also referred to as 'resorts') and motels, villas, apartments and campsites now serve the millions who flock to the area each year. At the last count there were nearly 80,000 rooms available in Orlando. Many hotels concentrate on the family holiday trade, offering excellent facilities and special deals for children. Others are heavily involved in Orlando's burgeoning convention business, and are sometimes too vast and impersonal to be welcoming. Some complexes cover such acreages that electric carts are provided to get around.

While prices vary widely, depending on the facilities available, the vast majority of Orlando hotels outside Walt Disney World are unmemorable modern blocks, one very much the same as the next. The criteria for choosing one rather than another are simple: location and price. Do not expect much discernible character or individuality. Virtually all the USA's major accommodation chains are represented in Orlando, many by more than one hotel. These may be run by different franchisees, so if you have pre-booked accommodation, make sure you know the exact name and address of your hotel.

There are perhaps 16 Days Inns in Orlando, half a dozen Holiday Inns, several Howard Johnsons. Other budget or middle-range chain names you will see constantly as you travel around the area are Ramada, Radisson, Travelodge, EconoLodge, Inns of America, Economy Inns, Best Western, Comfort Inn, and Quality Inn. Sheratons, Hiltons and Marriotts are pricier, more geared to the conference market.

While many hotel or motel buildings are lamentably crude boxes of rendered cement, standards inside are generally high. Even the cheapest motel rooms have full bathrooms (showers and baths, though not bidets) and enough bedspace for four people. You can almost invariably expect a large TV with bewildering opportunities for channel-zapping, a direct-dial telephone, and air-conditioning. Pricier places may have video recorders or microwaves, while anything referred to as a 'suite' will have some kind of kitchen. Surprisingly, amid all this gadgetry, bedrooms rarely have hairdryers, except in the most expensive hotels.

Fresh-air fiends will be unhappy: most American hotel rooms are hermetically double-glazed against traffic noise, intruders, insects and the intense summer heat, and you cannot open any of the windows. Stale cigarette smoke, therefore, tends to linger even longer than usual – be sure to request a non-smoking room if this is something which bothers you.

ACCOMMODATION

Out of season (that is, any time American children are safely penned up in school), there is a surplus of accommodation, and it is always worth asking for a discount. You can get some very good deals – perhaps as little as $20 for a perfectly decent double room. Some motel chains offer free accommodation, or free meals, for children, and there are cheaper rates for senior citizens too. If you belong to the American Automobile Association (the 'Triple A'), you can get discounts in a number of chains, usually around 10 per cent.

Choosing Where to Stay

The first decision to make if Orlando is your destination is whether or not you want to stay within Walt Disney World. If you do so, you will almost certainly pay more for your holiday overall, but there are considerable advantages. With their distinctive 'themed' architecture, glossy facilities, entertainment programmes, and highly trained staff, Disney hotels aim to give guests a complete holiday experience – that is, to be much more than mere bed-factories. You also get convenient transport and access to the Disney attractions (so you will not necessarily need to hire a car), and various privileges and discounts denied to those staying outside WDW. Disney promotional literature understandably emphasises these perks, and tends to ignore any benefits of staying (indeed, of doing anything at all!) outside the site.

The attractions of Walt Disney World are so many and varied that some visitors are quite content to spend all their holiday just doing Disney things. On the other hand you may find yourself wondering what goes on beyond the compound. Walt Disney World is by no means all that Orlando has to offer, and if you plan to stay longer than a week you may need a rest from Mickey and his little friends.

If you choose to stay outside WDW, you will almost certainly need a car (even if you stay on site, a rental car is highly recommended). Even the hotels advertised as 'right next to the Maingate entrance' are still miles away from the theme park turnstiles, so huge is the Disney complex.

Staying within the Walt Disney World resort

Within the confines of this vast theme park complex lie over twenty large hotels. Several of these function as self-contained resorts. Most of these hotels are actually owned and run by the Disney organisation; others (the World Dolphin and World Swan, and the seven on the Hotel Plaza near the Village) are leased or owned by other companies, but run strictly in accordance with the Disney ethos, right down to the receptionists' nail-polish! Alternative WDW accommodation consists of a large group of villas (Village Resort), and a camping ground called Fort Wilderness covering 780 acres (316 ha). See **Camping** in the **Directory**, page 114.

The Grand Floridian Beach Resort

All the Disney properties are extremely comfortable, imaginatively designed and pleasantly located in spacious, beautifully landscaped grounds. Needless to say, these luxury properties are not cheap, and high-season prices are awesome. None the less, most Disney accommodation is fully booked during peak holiday periods.

Staying outside WDW
Accommodation outside Walt Disney World is concentrated in two main areas. Highway 192, which runs east-west past the southern Maingate entrance to Walt Disney World towards the community of Kissimmee, is packed with hotels and motels. It is a noisy, busy road, and the development along it, as along most highways in Orlando, is hardly picturesque. The further away you are from Walt Disney World, the cheaper the tariffs, so if you are prepared to drive a few miles you can certainly

pick up a good bargain along here, especially out of season. Most of the other accommodation lies north-east of Walt Disney World, in the corridor of the main Interstate Highway (I-4) which runs directly (usually uncongested) towards downtown Orlando. There is a large concentration of hotels along International Drive, just east of I-4 – with its numerous attractions, a popular and convenient area to stay. Others lie further east on Sand Lake Road, the Orange Blossom Trail, and around the international airport. From these areas there are quite a few traffic-laden miles to drive to reach WDW.
There is plenty of accommodation in central Orlando too, mostly in unexceptional if perfectly comfortable business hotels. But the advantages or attractions of staying hemmed in by buildings this far from

the main sights are very limited – except perhaps in high season, when lower prices and occupancy rates may be worth considering. Further afield, a couple of hotels are appealing and unusual enough to consider as more than merely a bed for the night. One is in Winter Park, north of Orlando (Park Plaza), the other in Lakeland to the west, near the Cypress Gardens (Chalet Suzanne). See page 101, **Treats outside Orlando**, for details of these two.

Accommodation inside Walt Disney World

Resort Hotels and Villas
All Disney hotels are recommendable for their facilities and high standards of comfort. But they all have a different feel, and a different price tag – high, or very high! Cheapest rates are available at the Caribbean Beach Resort, and the new Port Orleans and Dixie Landings Hotels. Individual room-rates vary depending on the view, rather than the quality of the facilities. Location is also a consideration, though wherever you stay within Walt Disney World, efficient free transport is available. Three of the four Magic Kingdom resort hotels lie on the shores of the Seven Seas Lagoon, and are conveniently linked by the monorail system. These are the Grand Floridian Beach, the Contemporary, and the Polynesian Resorts. The EPCOT Center resorts are the Caribbean Beach, the Yacht Club and Beach Club, and the

World Dolphin and World Swan. Disney Village resorts include the suite hotel (Village Resort), plus Dixie Landing (tel: 934 6000) and Port Orleans (tel: 934 5000) with their Old South themes. Disney's newest hotel is the Animal Kingdom Lodge, where most balconies look over a savannah–like animal reserve (tel: 938 3000). There are seven other, more traditional, hotels nearby (see Hotel Plaza, page 98). For advance bookings at all these properties, contact **WDW Central Reservations**, Box 10100, Lake Buena Vista 32830, tel: 407-W DISNEY (934 7639). **Grand Floridian Resort and Spa** (tel: 824 3000). Victorian-looking turrets, gables and bargeboards characterise this rambling, red-roofed complex. Striking features include a soaring five-storey lobby, where colossal chandeliers hover beneath domes of stained glass, and rare birds twitter in an aviary. Big Bertha, a fairground organ, regales visitors in one of the restaurants. **Contemporary Resort** (tel: 824 1000). This vast concrete A-frame structure catches the eye (rather excessively) all round the Magic Kingdom. The monorail disappears inside it, dropping visitors off right by the lobby. Some find the architecture and style of this hotel alienating. Inside, the multi-storey car park atmosphere wears off gradually; the vertiginous heights of the atrium dwindle into people-scale compartments, and the decor is certainly imaginative.

Many bedrooms are in low-rise garden wings outside the tower block.

Polynesian Resort (tel: 824 2000). South Pacific motifs prevail. Visitors check in at the Great Ceremonial House, where tropical vegetation drips into a maze of pools and fountains. 'Longhouses' named after exotic islands stretch round the grounds, oddly drab with their brown, corrugated-iron-look roofing. At night, the gardens come alive with flaming gas torches, and lilting 'luau' music wafts across the soft white-sand beaches.

Caribbean Beach Resort (tel: 934 3400). A very extensive complex made up of a confection of separate, prettily designed, low-rise 'villages' (Aruba, Barbados, Jamaica, Martinique and Trinidad), each rendered in a different colour, with its own pool and little artificial lake-beach. Check in at the colonial-style Custom House, shop in the Calypso Trading Post or dine in a food-court at Old Port Royale. Lots of entertainment and an island play area for kids. Cheerful staff redirect you when you are lost. One of the most attractive and best-value Disney hotel properties.

The **All Star Sports Hotel** (tel: 939 5000) is a more budget orientated addition near the Epcot Center. The All Star Sports has 1,900 rooms and was the first phase of the 'All Star Village Resort' including the All Star Music and All Star Movie Hotels. Moderate prices.

Wilderness Lodge (tel: 939 5100) is a 729-room luxury hotel situated in the forest at Bay Lake, between Fort Wilderness and the Magic Kingdom. Coaches and motor launches take guests to the entertainment parks.

Yacht and **Beach Club Resorts** (tel: 934 7000 and 934 8000 respectively). These two hotels effectively function as one, though they do have distinct 'themes'. Externally the only difference between their Eastern Seaboard architecture is the colour: oyster-grey for the Yacht Club; harebell-blue for the Beach Club. The Yacht Club goes for nautical décor inside, all brass rails and gleaming mahogany; the Beach Club is a slice of old New England, clapboard and clam chowder. A particularly nice feature is the waterfront and white-sand beach, and a fantasy lagoon inside a mock shipwreck, where you can swim alongside the freshwater fish, or even hurtle down waterslides.

World Swan and **World Dolphin Hotels** (tel: 934 3000 and 934 4000 respectively). Though leased and operated by two different companies (Westin and Sheraton), these magnificently eccentric buildings were simultaneously designed both inside and out by the architect Michael Graves, and are very similar in size and concept. They now make eye-catching twin landmarks all around EPCOT. As fantastic externally as anything in Walt Disney World, their bold facades look like painted film-sets, one all waves and giant swans, the other graced by a vast shell waterfall tumbling down its side, huge urns and 55-foot (17-metre) dolphins. Inside, the fantasy continues with Egyptian motifs, pineapples, and monkey chandeliers. Like them or not, in a world of standardised construction these hotels are a breath of fresh air.

Village Resort (tel: 827 1100). Five well-equipped types of villa are available on this extensive site near the Marketplace, sleeping from four to six adults. They range from one-bedroomed Vacation Villas to the luxury Grand Vista Suites or the intriguing Treehouse Villas on stilts in a pinewood. Facilities and furnishings are of a very high standard, and for families of 5-plus they represent an interesting option. Lots of sports amenities are available on site, including golf, swimming, tennis, fishing and boating. To get around you can hire bikes or electric carts, or use the free bus network. The Gourmet Pantry provides groceries (free delivery service).

Hotel Plaza

The other group of hotels within WDW lies to the east, in the section called Walt Disney World Village. Along the Hotel Plaza Boulevard stand seven large hotel blocks. Guests who stay here enjoy the same privileges as other Disney clients, such as free use of the transport system throughout the parks, priority bookings for dinner shows, use of Village Clubhouse sports facilities, and so on. The hotels are the gleaming tower-block Buena Vista Palace, the Grosvenor Resort, the Hilton, the Howard Johnson Resort, the Royal Plaza, a Travelodge and a massive suite complex known as the Guest Quarters. These are the two we liked best: **Hilton**, 1751 Hotel Plaza Boulevard, Lake Buena Vista (tel: 827 4000 or fax 827 3890). This wide-angled slab of concrete looks somewhat daunting from outside. It is, of course, smoothly geared to the business executive trade, with many state-of-the-art facilities and prices to suit. But it caters well for families with children too: Hilton's Youth Hotel's supervised programme is available to take them off your hands for a while. Public areas are bland but user-friendly. Good-value self-service buffet.

Grosvenor Resort, 1850 Hotel Plaza Boulevard, Lake Buena Vista (tel: 828 4444 or fax 828 8192). Easily one of the most attractive and personal hotels in this complex, with an agreeable mix of family and corporate trade. Though less expensive than the Hilton, it is no budget option, but its excellent location and views, comfortable bedrooms and friendliness of staff make it one of the best value. Decor is handsome: a vaguely 19th-century colonial feel in pastel shades. A special feature is the Sherlock Holmes museum in one of its restaurants, a recreation of 221B Baker Street, London – legendary home of Sir Arthur Conan Doyle's famous sleuth.

Accommodation outside Walt Disney World

International Drive Area

Expensive

Peabody Orlando, 9801 International Drive (tel: 352 4000). This daunting high-rise hotel stands in spacious grounds at the classier, southern end of 'The Drive'. More appealing than the lavish interior and predictably luxurious facilities are its impeccable standards of service and friendly, personal attention. The Peabody's most winsome feature, though, is an unexpected tribe of resident mallards. Every morning, at 11.00hrs, a drake and his four wives waddle before their keeper along a red carpet to splash away the day in the marble lobby fountain, then march back again at 17.00hrs. The Duck March has now achieved the status of a local tourist attraction. If you can afford it, this is a fine hotel to be pampered in. If not, at least go and say hello to the ducks!
Portofino Bay, 5601,000 Universal Boulevard (tel: 224 7117 or 837 2273; www.uescape.com).
This is a lovely hotel, attached to and part of the new Universal Orlando, with 795 luxurious rooms and suites in a pretty pastel Italian-themed resort. There are great facilities including pools, dining and a health club. CityWalk is not far away. Guests recieve benefits such as early entry into the Universal parks, similar to Walt Disney Hotels.

Moderate

Heritage Inn Orlando, 9861 International Drive (tel: 352 0008). Rockers on the front porch lend an air of relaxed southern hospitality to this attractive, plantation-style hotel next to the Peabody. Inside, brass chandeliers, dark wood fittings and paddle fans evoke the charm of 19th-century Florida, and bedrooms have colonial touches. Theatre dinners feature several times a week in the big circular dining hall. The Golden Tulip connection makes it a popular venue for Dutch guests. A complimentary shuttle bus takes you to the attractions.

The Peabody Orlando

ACCOMMODATION

Delta Orlando Resort, 5715 Major Boulevard (tel: 351 3340). Low-rise blocks, functional but unobtrusive, stand in peaceful, spacious grounds just a stone's throw from Universal Studios (complimentary shuttle). Bedrooms show signs of wear in places, but the pool terrace, adventure playground, and mini-golf course are pleasant, staff are friendly, and the tariff is very good value.

Inexpensive
Holiday Inn Sunspree Resort Lake Buena Vista, 13351 SR 535 (off I-4) (tel: 239 4500). This is a popular, family-friendly hotel. Children are greeted by the hotel's mascots, a pair of raccoons named Max and Maxine, and check in at their own desk, where they receive a bag of goodies. The rooms are of the dependable chain-hotel variety, but they are larger than average and have kitchenettes. Families can also choose to book a 'kids' suite', decorated in various themes that include an igloo and a boat.

Highway 192

Moderate
Ramada Resort Maingate, 2950 Reedy Creek Boulevard, Kissimmee (tel: 240 7100 for reservations or 396 4466 for hotel reception). One of the closest off-site hotels to Walt Disney World, this unobtrusive building shows no great promise from outside, but is quietly set back from the main highway overlooking the woodlands of WDW and its own small gardens and pool. Decor

(pale blue rattan and blondwood in public areas; tasteful modern fabrics in bedrooms) is light and inoffensive; rooms are spacious and well equipped. In common with several hotels close by, a free shuttle bus service operates regularly to WDW.
Holiday Inn Maingate West #2, 7601 Black Lake Road, Kissimmee (tel: 396 1100). Check the address and your compass (close by there is also a Holiday Inn Maingate, and a Holiday Inn Maingate East – all, incidentally, run by different companies) for this pink-washed building set back from Highway 192, less than two miles (3km) west of WDW's main entrance. As with many local hotels, its box-like exterior belies the high standards of furnishings within and its general air of quietness. Staff are helpful; the plant-filled foyer lounge and Palms restaurant cool and relaxing.
Holiday Inn Maingate, 7300 Irlo Bronson Highway, Kissimmee (tel: 396 7300). Though the roadside block opposite WDW's Maingate entrance looks uninvitingly close to the highway, its large, tasteful bedrooms are well insulated, and rear rooms are right away from the traffic. Do not necessarily expect a quiet life, however: this hotel caters particularly for families with children, with stacks of entertainment, playgrounds and paddling pools, and child-oriented fast food.
Sol Orlando, 4787 West Irlo Bronson Memorial Highway, Kissimmee (tel: 397 0555).

Spanish-style villas in a secluded, attractive complex well back from the road. Public areas (a well-furnished lobby and restaurant) have more personality than most, and the pantiled bedroom wings are comfortable and civilised.

Inexpensive
Hostelling International Oralndo/Kissimmee Resort, 4840 W. Irlo Bronson, Kissimmee (tel: 396 8282). Great facilities including a beautiful swimming pool, two acres of tropical grounds and a barbeque. Access is available 24 hours and rooms don't have more than six beds. Well-placed for Walt Disney World.

Treats outside Orlando
Park Plaza, 307 Park Avenue South, Winter Park (tel: 647 1072). One of very few hotels in Orlando that counts as intimate, personal, and genuinely classy. In an up-market residential suburb of North Orlando, the hotel overlooks Central Park and the smart shopping street of Park Avenue. No two of its 27 rooms are the same, though all are decorated and furnished with equal panache. Antiques and oriental rugs grace bedrooms festooned with plants, whirling fans and white wickerwork. Outside some of these elegant, comfortable rooms runs a balcony where you can take your complimentary continental breakfast amid fern-laden hanging baskets. Staff are unfailingly helpful and courteous, and the food in the Gardens restaurant is something to remember (see

Every comfort can be found at Chalet Suzanne

Restaurants, page 78).
Chalet Suzanne, US27S (exit 17A), 3800 Chalet Suzanne Drive, Lake Wales, FL33853 (tel: 941 676 6011). You find this unusual restaurant and country inn in Orlando's Lakeland, as you head for the Cypress Gardens or the Bok Tower Gardens. This whimsical Florida mansion seems to have stepped out of some gentle, old-fashioned Disney animation, its 30 charmingly folksy bedrooms scattered through a village-like complex of cottages and mini-castles. Opened during the Depression by its enterprising, newly widowed doyenne, Chalet Suzanne is now a smart enough venue to require a private landing strip in its lake-and-woodland grounds amid the citrus groves. The gourmet food is a strong point: well worth a trek for dinner in its elegantly cluttered restaurant even if you are not staying here (see **Restaurants**, page 75).

NIGHTLIFE AND ENTERTAINMENT

Entertainment in Orlando does not stop as darkness falls, but, like the rest of the region's attractions, it is very much geared to families and is almost always wholesome enough for the most sensitive child or maiden aunt. The big theme parks (Magic Kingdom, EPCOT Center, Sea World and Universal Orlando) end the day with some kind of spectacular pageant. The attractions of Church Street Station and Pleasure Island really come to life in the evenings, though the shops and restaurants stay open all day (for details, see the separate entries). Dinner shows and evening cruises are tourist-circuit staples, and many hotels and restaurants provide live entertainment of some sort. For discos, head downtown to **J J Whispers**, on Lee Road. You can find rock and roll at **Little Darlin's**, off US192, in Kissimmee. Winter Park boasts a few chic bars and clubs for the smart set, such as the Crocodile Club at **Bailey's Restaurant** (West Fairbanks Avenue), and **Sullivan's Trailways Lounge** is a good place for dancing. Pick up the local newspaper, the *Orlando Sentinel*, for weekly 'what's on' listings, or telephone the Arts Hotline on 420 2150 for information. Ballet, opera and dance companies and orchestras perform seasonally on tour. Orlando's main theatres are at **Loch Haven Park**, and **Rollins College**, Winter Park.

Walt Disney World Nightlife

The Disney folk hang on to their customers as long as possible by ending each day at the parks with a loud bang: fireworks and lasers in EPCOT Center; a water pageant and a parade of brightly lit electrical floats bearing Disney characters in the Magic Kingdom. Both these regular events are very colourful and exciting for children, and it is worth staying till closing time to catch them. Disney's specialist nightspot is **Pleasure Island**, near the Village, a waterfront stage-set of wharfs and warehouses where New Year's Eve is celebrated nightly with a continuous whoopee of shows and disco dancing (more fully described on page 48). Several 'official' Disney hotels in the Village (see **Hotel Plaza**, page 98) have nightspots: the **Buena Vista Palace** has a flashy nightclub called the Laughing Kookaburra; the **Royal Plaza** has the Giraffe Lounge disco and La Cantina guitar bar; the **Grosvenor** offers murder and mystery evenings in its Sherlock Holmes themed restaurant, Baskervilles, and the Moriarty pub. Dinner shows are regularly held at several Disney resorts, the most popular of which is at Fort Wilderness. Book up quickly if you want to catch the *Hoop-Dee-Doo Musical Revue* at the Pioneer Hall in Fort Wilderness, a sort of giant log cabin. Audiences munch through a hefty meal of honeyed corn, barbecued spare ribs, baked beans, chicken pieces and strawberry shortcake, interspersed with

Country and Western song and dance routines and corny wisecracks. The enthusiasm of the entertainers is infectious and astonishing, considering they do the same show three times a night (at 17.00, 19.15 and 21.45hrs) to packed houses. Dress casual.

The Contemporary Resort's Top of the World restaurant on the 15th floor provides a smart, formal setting for a pretty good dinner and *Broadway at the Top* – a big band medley of hits from great Broadway shows of yesteryear (Andrew Lloyd Webber plays a significant, unacknowledged part). No marks for originality, but snazzy costumes, good dancing and lots of pizazz.

The Polynesian Revue is a gentle South Pacific 'luau' show down by the white-sand tropical cove of the Polynesian Resort, with music, flower garlands, native hula dancing, and a barbecue. It is a nice but not particularly gripping event,

incidentally rivalled by Sea World's similar evening cabaret. An afternoon show at 16.30hrs called *Mickey's Tropical Revue* brings Disney characters into a south-sea context for the children.

Dinner Shows outside WDW
Among the showers of leaflets advertising Orlando's attractions you are bound to encounter news of these popular nightly spectacles, often included in holiday packages.
King Henry's Feast, held in a mock-Tudor palace, 8984 International Drive (tel: 351 5151), is one of the best-paced and most entertaining of these uproarious themed dinner shows. Diners sit round a raised dais from which the king and his jester select a lucky seventh, or even an eighth prospective 'wife' from the audience. Wenches serve the chicken joints and spare ribs and endlessly flowing

Everyone's a performer, it seems

NIGHTLIFE AND ENTERTAINMENT

Catastrophe Canyon, on Disney-MGM's Backstage Studio Tour

drink; sword-fighting knights, jugglers and minstrels keep the show rolling. The acts are well rehearsed, the jester amiably impertinent, the king a great showman.

Arabian Nights, 6225 West Irlo Bronson Memorial Highway, Kissimmee (tel: 239 9223). Scheherezade searches for her prince in an enormous arena covered in wood-chip fibre, but the stars of this show are the Arabian and Lippizaner horses who perform dancing and leaping acrobatics. The programme includes a Ben Hur chariot race, a superb black stallion, and a prime-rib dinner. Some acts need more rehearsal, but this show is well liked by many visitors.

Medieval Times A Spanish-style pageant of horsemanship, falconry, swordplay and jousting in a fake castle on Highway 192, Kissimmee (tel: 396 1518). Audience participation approaches deafening levels as their chosen knights compete on classy Andalucian horses, and

distribute carnation favours. The jousting acts are impressively performed, and the roast chicken dinner (eaten with your fingers, of course) appetising.

Other dinner shows widely advertised include a Wild West-style romp at **Fort Liberty**, 5260 Highway 192, Kissimmee (tel: 351 5151); a carnival scene at **Mardi Gras**, The Mercado, 8445 International Drive (tel: 351 5151); an Oriental evening at **Asian Adventure**, 5225 International Drive (tel: 351 5655); a whodunnit mystery show called **Sleuths**, 7508 Universal Boulevard (tel: 363 1985); and a steamboat cruise on the *Grand Romance* rivership, based in Sanford (see page 79).

Most of these evening entertainments are quite expensive ($30–40), and the food suffers the fate of most mass catering, but try at least one while you are there.

WEATHER AND WHEN TO GO

During the summer (late May to September), midday temperatures in central Florida soar into the mid-30sC (90sF), accompanied by intense humidity and thunderous rainstorms. The rest of the year the heat is more bearable, somewhere in the 16–21°C (60sF) or mid-20sC (70sF), though night-time lows can sink into the 10–15°C (50sF), and, as those withered citrus groves around Orlando indicate, quite severe winter frosts are not unknown. Temperatures inland are more variable than on the Florida coast, which is tempered by the Gulf Stream. On the other hand, the violent hurricanes that sometimes batter coastal districts during the late summer have usually moderated to ill-tempered squalls by the time they reach Walt Disney World, and serious storm damage is rare. The wettest months in Orlando are June, July, August and September, which, combined with the heat, can be quite oppressive. It is dryest from November to January. Early morning fog can present a hazard to drivers at certain times of year.

What to Wear

If you visit Orlando during summer, take precautions against the sun. Queueing for rides in those temperatures is no joke, and it is particularly important to keep an eye on young children, who quickly wilt in the heat. Wear a hat and an effective sunscreen, even in the winter months, whenever you are spending long periods outside. Take a light cagoule or folding umbrella with you into the parks; almost every afternoon in summer the blue skies blacken for a brief but thoroughly drenching shower. Whenever this happens a flurry of bright yellow Mickey ponchos miraculously appears on every Disney shop counter for the foolish virgins who have left their raincoats in the car park.

Dress codes in Orlando are casual, with comfort being the prime consideration. Loose cotton T-shirts, shorts, and trainers may not suit everyone, but you will quickly discover why the vast majority of American visitors virtually live in this relaxed garb while exploring the theme parks. Too much stripping off, however, is frowned on: quaint notices at Walt Disney World inform visitors that shirts and shoes are

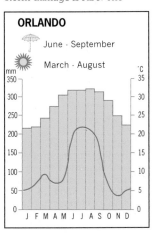

ORLANDO

June · September

March · August

obligatory. At any time of year, take a light jacket or sweater for cool evenings, or over-zealous air-conditioning. Smarter hotels and eating places may insist that men wear a jacket, though ties are rarely required. By far the most important item of clothing to take, however, is a pair of thoroughly comfortable shoes. You will spend many hours regretting it if you don't!

When to Go

Ideally, avoid the American school holidays. This may not be practical advice if you have children of school age, but Walt Disney World becomes hideously overcrowded at Easter, Christmas and New Year, and the major public holidays such as Thanksgiving (3rd week in November), Washington's Birthday (mid-February), and of course 4 July. Any time from mid-June to late August is also more than usually crowded with families, as is the spring break in late March. From Christmas to Easter, the winter season, Florida's mild weather attracts long-stay visitors from northerly states, many of whom have second homes in Florida. Special events, such as space launches, also attract a sudden influx of visitors. Late spring and autumn (April/May, or October to mid-December) are good times to go: crowds are lighter, queues shorter, accommodation cheaper and easier to book, and temperatures much pleasanter for exploring. During quiet times, however, you may find some of the attractions

closed for renovation, and the parks shut early, without the colourful evening parades and firework shows.

Oddly enough, tourist patterns in the USA mean that weekends are not the most crowded days in the parks. In fact, Fridays and Sundays are quietest of all, Thursdays and Saturdays quite good, and Mondays, Tuesdays and Wednesdays the busiest. Whichever day you go, however, get to the parks early – at least half an hour before the official opening time – and make the most of cooler, quieter mornings for the most popular rides.

HOW TO BE A LOCAL

All you need to do to mesh with central Florida is relax, abandon inhibitions, and have a nice day! Orlando is not for the standoffish or painfully shy, or for those seeking meaningful cultural experiences. Just about everyone there is some sort of tourist, so everything is geared towards you, and towards having a continuous round of rollicking, childish fun. Native Floridians are naturally easy-going and friendly, and the pace of life is southern and slowish. Add to that the polished smiles of Walt Disney World's employees, and you would have to be churlish indeed to feel unhappy. Just one note of caution: Florida is a tolerant but conservative place, and behaviour that offends the respectable sensibilities of family-oriented Middle America is out. That includes stripping off by the pool, public drunkenness and drug abuse.

CHILDREN

Most of this book is dedicated to children – that is, to the child in all of us. Parents pretend they are taking their offspring to Orlando's theme parks, but they emerge from the rides grinning like jackasses, unwilling to admit how much they have enjoyed themselves. Walt Disney World caters magnificently for children of all ages, as do most of Orlando's attractions, hotels and restaurants.

Child-care facilities at Walt Disney World and the other main theme parks include playgrounds, games rooms, crèches and day-care centres, name tags (in case they get lost), strollers (pushchairs) rentable for $4–5 a day, nappy-changing and feeding rooms, baby-sitters, cots, bibs and high-chairs, and a large stock of all kinds of baby equipment, books and toys on sale. There is an efficient, vigilant system of rounding up children who have strayed, and Mickey and his friends are constantly on hand to entertain and cheer up their young fans. Guest services desks in all the parks can give information about facilities for children.

The Stress Factor

You have paid a lot of money, travelled a long way, and your expectations are somewhere in orbit. The children are excited, and terribly overtired. You have bought a pass for an arm and a leg, but you only have a few days to spare, and there is an awful lot to see. The queues look awesome, and the sun beats down. Somehow, you must fight your way in and enjoy yourselves. Just the time for trouble. No sooner through the turnstiles, and the wails begin. The size and scale of Orlando's attractions can place a lot of pressure on small children – and their keepers. Rule one, get them in a good frame of mind before you start. Keep things relaxed and low key. You may plan the day with military precision, but don't convey this to the kids. Make an early start, but don't worry if

A holiday for children of all ages

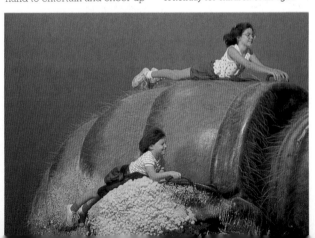

everyone needs a break at some point. Have lunch, or leave the parks altogether and go back to your hotel for a swim and a rest if it is not too far – you can return later if you get a hand-stamp of invisible fluorescent ink as you leave. Check the individual entries in this book for approximate guidelines on how suitable individual attractions are for different age ranges. It is impossible to predict children's reactions accurately, however. They may take the wildest roller-coaster completely in their stride, then become strangely alarmed at some innocuous fibreglass monster.

Meeting Mickey

A visit to Walt Disney World would not be complete without at least one close personal encounter with Mickey.The best place to find the Disney characters is Mickey's Starland, in the Magic Kingdom, but you will see them during afternoon parades too (best viewpoint is Frontierland), or catch them over 'Character breakfasts' at several of the resort hotels.

Education or Entertainment?

Despite worthy enterprises such as EPCOT Center, the educational element at Walt Disney World and the other theme parks is limited. Children are too bombarded with sensations to take in much information. So if you have taken your children out of school to visit Orlando, don't fool yourself they are learning a lot. It's fun, great fun, but not much else.

TIGHT BUDGET

Orlando throbs with temptations to spend money at every turn, and it is painfully easy to let more dollars trickle through your fingers than you anticipated, particularly if you have impulsive children in tow. Some things are relatively inexpensive by European standards: petrol, car hire, food and accommodation – if carefully chosen. But that 6 per cent sales tax (nearly always added on top of the prices displayed, except essential food items), and the pointed reminders that gratuities (usually between 15 and 20 per cent) are not included in the bill, can make unexpected dents in your budget. In addition, a resort tax of between 2 and 4 per cent is levied on hotel bills.

● Visit Orlando out of high season, when package prices, hotel costs, car hire and entrance charges may be much lower. Ask for a discount if your hotel is plainly not full. Competition is fierce at slack periods.

● Prioritise attraction visits carefully. Decide what you want to see and do in the time available, and stick to your plans. Some of Orlando's minor diversions represent poor value for money.

● Car hire costs vary widely, and local dealers may be cheaper than big international companies. Collision damage waiver and adequate insurance are essential, but the gold-plated insurance cover some companies try to sell you is very expensive, and generally unnecessary (see **Driving,** page 115).

● Choose accommodation carefully; you will pay for posh facilities, whether you use them or not. Remember that most bedrooms sleep at least four people, and the price stays the same. If you have a large party, consider renting a villa or condominium.

● Some hotels and restaurants (especially the chains) offer special deals for children (they stay or eat free), or senior citizens, but age limits and periods of application vary. Some hotels offer discounts of around 10 per cent to members of the American Automobile Association. Check also the free tourist newspapers and leaflets, which often contain worthwhile discount coupons.

● Use tea- and coffee-making facilities in hotels, and the ice machines for supermarket cold drinks, rather than constantly paying bar and restaurant prices.

● Avoid expensive telephone calls from hotel bedrooms. There is often a 75 per cent mark-up on long-distance calls, and that is not very far in Orlando – the region spans three separate counties.

● Meal portions are nearly always very generous. Order just one course to start with, and see how hungry you are afterwards. Lunches in smarter restaurants are usually less costly than dinners; or you could skip lunch altogether and have a hefty brunch.

● Many cocktail bars have a 'Happy Hour' somewhere

The Python, Busch Gardens

between 17.30 and 19.30hrs. Drinks are half-price, with enough free canapés and snacks to stave off evening hunger pangs.

● Diners, fast-food chains and self-service cafés are more economical places to stoke up than big hotels. Look out for inclusive 'all-you-can-eat' prices, and cheaper 'early bird' dinner menus before 17.00 or 18.00hrs.

● Cut down on the incidentals: snacks, ice-creams and souvenirs soon mount up with a family.

● Shop at factory outlets such as Belz, or markets such as Flea World (see **Shopping,** pages 90–92).

● While it is important not to dehydrate in Florida's hot sunshine, repeated rounds of soft drinks are expensive and calorific, and may cause stomach chills. Make use of the drinking-water fountains liberally placed throughout the big theme parks. They are hygienic, fast, unfattening – and free!

● There is a premium on stamps if you buy them from a slot machine, though you see these everywhere. Get them from post offices (rather few and far between), or Walt Disney World hotels.

● A word of warning on booths selling 'discount' Walt Disney World tickets. These are very often a front for time-share dealers, and you may be inveigled into inspecting some property or other.

● Two of Orlando's main through-routes (the Beeline Expressway and Florida's Turnpike) are toll roads. The only time you really need them is if you are dashing for a plane, or hammering off to Miami. The I-75 is a useful alternative north–south route, rather than the Turnpike, and will also take you to Miami.

Spills at the Silver Spurs Rodeo

SPECIAL EVENTS

Central Florida's energetic tourist carousel revolves with a year-round programme of festivals, sports events and party celebrations, especially at holiday times. It is easy to find out what is going on from local newspapers, free visitor guides and stacks of promotional leaflets fluttering around hotel lobbies and other public places. For more details or reservations, contact guest relations staff at tourist hotels and theme parks, or the Orlando/Orange County Convention and Visitors Bureau at 8445 International Drive (in the Mercado Mediterranean Village, tel: 363 5871). Some of the main regular annual fixtures are listed below.

January
New Year Celebrations, Walt Disney World; Florida Citrus Bowl Football Classic, Orlando Stadium; Scottish Highland Games, Central Florida Fairgrounds.

February
Disney Village Wine Festival;Black Hills Passion Play, Lake Wales; Central Florida Fair, Central Florida Fairgrounds; Silver Spurs Rodeo, Kissimmee (also takes place in July).

March
Houston Astros Spring Training (baseball), Osceola County Stadium, Kissimmee; Kissimmee Bluegrass Festival; Nestlé International PGA Tour (golf), Bay Hill Club; St Patrick's Day Street Party, Church Street Station; Winter Park Sidewalk Art Festival.

April
Orlando Sunrays baseball
season begins (April–August);
Easter Parades at WDW.
May
Up, Up and Away Airport Art
Show, Orlando International
Airport.
June
Kissimmee Boat-a-Cade, Lake
Tohopekaliga.
July
Silver Spurs Rodeo, Kissimmee;
Fourth of July Celebrations,
WDW.
September
Osceola Art Festival, Lake Toho
(Tohopekaliga), Kissimmee;
Oktoberfest (really!), Church
Street Station; Autofest, Old
Town, Kissimmee (classic cars).
October
Pioneer Days (folk festival),
Pine Castle Folk Art Center;
Florida State Air Fair,
Kissimmee; Kissimmee Boating
Jamboree, Lake Toho;
Oldsmobile Golf Classic, WDW;
Hallowe'en celebrations
throughout Orlando.
November
Festival of Masters (art show),
Disney Village Marketplace;
Light Up Orlando (street party),
downtown Orlando.
December
Pet Fair, Loch Haven Park; Half-
marathon, Lake Eola Park;
Christmas Celebrations, WDW.

SPORT

Sports facilities are an important
aspect of central Florida's status
as a complete holiday
playground. Those available at
Walt Disney World alone are
impressive enough, but outside
Mouseland there are stacks

All-weather courts are available

more. Orlando's vast number of
lakes and rivers provide a
venue for inland watersports,
but should you crave salt and
surf it is only an hour or so's
easy drive to either coastline.
Tuition and equipment hire are
easily arranged; bring suitable
clothes. For more information,
phone the **Orlando Recreation
Department** on 363 5871.
Golf Walt Disney World has
five courses of its own: two near
the Disney Inn by the Magic
Kingdom, two near the Dixie
Landings Resort, north-east of
EPCOT Center, and one at Lake
Buena Vista. Green fees for
these mid-range championship
courses are quite expensive,
even for Disney guests. There
is also a six-hole course by
Lake Buena Vista. An important
annual event (for spectators
unless you are very keen and
very rich) is the WDW/
Oldsmobile Golf Classic
tournament in October. Within
easy range of Orlando are at
least eight other golf resorts.
Tennis The Contemporary
Resort, with six floodlit courts, is
a good bet for keen tennis

SPORT

players, but several other WDW resort hotels have hard courts (lessons can be arranged). Outside WDW, half a dozen centres have multiple all-weather floodlit courts, many free of charge.

Fishing Bass-fishing is one of central Florida's most popular sports. Bay Lake and the Seven Seas Lagoon in WDW permit strictly controlled two-hour fishing trips (no licence required). Fishing is free (and again no licence is required) in the waterways around Fort Wilderness Resort. If you have cooking facilities you can keep your fish; otherwise you just chuck the poor things back in for the next punter. Lots of other fishing camps organise trips, especially on Lake Toho, Kissimmee. A licence is required on all other Florida waters – for more information about fishing in the area, contact the regional office of the **Fish and Wildlife Conservation Commission**, 3900 Drane Field Road, Lakeland, FL 33811 (tel: 813 648 3202).

Watersports Many varied craft can be hired for use on WDW lakes: tiny powered water sprites, pedal boats, outrigger canoes, motor boats and sailing boats. One of the nicest watersports centres in Walt Disney World is River Country (see page 50). Outside WDW, several rural spots for camping, swimming and canoeing lie north of the city, along the Wekiva River. Whizzier watersports in Orlando include waterskiing, parasailing, boardsailing, and airboats (try Splash 'N' Ski, or Old-Fashioned Air Boat Rides). Luxury houseboats are available for hire on the St John's River. Most hotels in Orlando have some sort of swimming pool, whether it be a little motel puddle in hard, hot concrete, or the elaborate three-tiered fantasy at the Hyatt Regency Grand Cypress, complete with grottoes and waterfalls. If you are mad on swimming, head for WDW's beautifully landscaped Typhoon Lagoon (see pages 49–50), the high-tech tubular water-parks of Wet 'n Wild and Water Mania (see page 82), or the Radisson Inn Aquatic Center on International Drive.

Riding You can ride gentle, unthreatening mounts (age limit, 9 plus) at Disney's Fort Wilderness, more excitingly along old logging trails at Poinciana Horse World (tel: 847 4343) in Kissimmee, and several other stables.

Other Sports Ice-skating, bowling, jogging and cycling can also be arranged. Spectator sports include a Jai Alai centre and a dog-track north of Orlando, the Orlando Magic Basketball team, several baseball teams, and, of course, American football. Perhaps the most exciting sporting activity, available in several locations, is hot-air ballooning. Trips are not cheap, at around $150 per person, but the sight of these colourful craft slowly drifting across Orlando's dawn skyline is enchanting. Balloon Flights of Florida (tel: 407 841 8787) at Church Street Station is one of the most widely advertised companies, offering champagne breakfast trips.

Directory

This section (with the biscuit-coloured band) contains day-to-day information, including travel, health and documentation

Contents

Arriving

Orlando's international airport is one of the fastest growing in the US, handling over 18 million passengers annually, and around 800 flights a day. It has undergone a massive $800 million expansion programme which included the development of four terminals and runways. It is an efficient and pleasant airport, with an enterprising range of restaurants. Souvenir shops from the major theme parks give visitors a first chance to buy Mouse Ears and, needless to say, there is a Walt Disney World information centre. Over 24 carriers fly into Orlando, including scheduled flights with British Airways, Delta Air Lines, North-West, TWA, KLM, American, US Air, and Continental, plus many charters such as Britannia Airways and Caledonian Airways. Florida's alternative airports are at Tampa, about an hour and a half's drive away from Orlando, Miami or Sanford. From Orlando's airport, take the Beeline Expressway westwards for Walt Disney World or International Drive, where most tourists stay. It is a toll road, so have a couple of dollars of loose change handy. It is a bus route (costing around $10 single as far as International Drive); taxis are much more expensive ($35 or so). Some major hotels provide a complimentary shuttle service (others charge for it).

Travel Documents Many foreign visitors with a valid return ticket no longer require a visa to enter the US for stays (business or leisure) not exceeding 90 days (except Australians). All you need is a passport (British Visitors' Passport not acceptable). You may need a visa if you plan to leave the US at any point during your stay, such as a visit to Mexico or the Caribbean. Check with the US Embassy before you leave. You must complete a visa waiver form, which will be processed at your first entry point to the US. If you take a connecting flight, have your form ready for your first encounter with US immigration authorities, who like things in apple-pie order.

Camping

The great outdoors is as popular in Florida as anywhere in the States, and there is plenty of opportunity in and around Orlando for all kinds of year-round camping, whether in a simple tent, an 'RV' (Recreational Vehicle) or static trailer home with all mod cons. Walt Disney World devotes a huge 650-acre (263-ha) resort, **Fort Wilderness**, to camping, offering over 800 wooded sites for tents, RVs and luxuriously kitted Fleetwood Trailers with air-conditioning and huge TVs, cabins are also available (tel: 407 824 2900). There are stacks of sports, shops, and things to do on site. Alternatives include three widely advertised **Yogi** **Bear's Jellystone Park** sites, and the lakeside **Port 0' Call Campground** in Kissimmee. All these are large, with the sort of facilities that obviate any pressing need to experience nature at first hand. Simpler, more backwoodsy options can be found in the attractive Wekiva River area north of Orlando (log cabins to rent), or in Lakeland, to the west. The *Florida Camping Directory*, an annual publication, is available free from Florida Association of RV Parks and Campgrounds, 1340 Vickers Drive, Tallahassee FL32303 (tel: 850 562 7151). The American Automobile Association (AAA) also has a list of camping grounds.

Chemist see Pharmacies

Crime

Orlando's statistics show that crimes against non-residents are incredibly low. However it is always wise to be cautious. Money escapes from your pockets in lots of quite legitimate ways; otherwise, it is more likely to fall out as you are upside-down on a roller-coaster than anything else. Take obvious, sensible precautions: never carry too much loose cash; use hotel safes (usually provided free of charge to guests); lock and bolt your motel door. Miami's rich pickings have attracted many opportunist thieves, and if you plan a coastal excursion, be very vigilant. Get a good map and never stray into unsalubrious downtown sectors. The police, tourist office, or AAA can advise you on no-go areas.

115

Customs Regulations

Non-US residents aged 21 or
over can bring in up to a litre of
alcohol; 200 cigarettes or 50
cigars (or 100 non-Cuban
cigars) and gifts worth up to
$100. There are no currency
limits. Regulations on importing
meat products, seeds or plants
are very strict. That Cox's
Pippin you packed for the
connecting flight will be
humourlessly confiscated with a
stern reprimand. Just imagine
what they do with narcotics!

Disabled People

The major theme parks,
particularly Walt Disney World,
score very highly for their
thoughtful provision of facilities
for elderly and disabled
visitors. All but the wildest rides
are accessible, and highly
trained, friendly staff are always
on hand to help. Wheelchairs
can be rented inexpensively in
all the parks for anyone who
has difficulty in walking, and
wheelchair visitors are always
given priority in queues; most
restrooms (WCs), car parks,
lifts and entrances are sensibly
planned. Audio and visual aids
are available for sight- or
hearing-impaired visitors. A
free booklet, *The Disabled
Guest*, is available from Walt
Disney World (tel: 939 6244).

Driving

Americans drive on the right,
calculate distances in miles, and
buy petrol (gas) in US gallons
(slightly smaller than the
imperial measure). The road
system all around Orlando is
excellent, with well-maintained
four- and six-lane highways in
all directions. Even so, the

Downtown Orlando

sheer volume of visitors can
clog them up at peak periods,
and there is a significant rush-
hour factor in downtown
Orlando. The most useful road
in Orlando is Interstate Highway
4, known as I-4, which runs
from Tampa on the west coast
of Florida to Daytona on the
east. It is a fast, painless artery
bypass through Orlando and
the International Drive area to
Walt Disney World where most
of the attractions lie. Exits are
clearly marked. Get to know
them, and be compass-literate
– you need to know if you are
heading east or west. A couple
of highways in Orlando (the
Beeline Expressway (SR528)
leading to the airport, and the
north–south Florida's Turnpike)
are toll roads – avoid these
unless you are in a special
hurry. An alternative
north–south route, rather than
the Turnpike, is the I-75.
Driving techniques in the US

are different from those in Europe. Most vehicles proceed sedately, sticking to the (fairly low) speed limits, constantly in the same lane. You can overtake on either side, but unnecessary lane-hopping is ill advised. Sometimes extreme right- or left-hand lanes are for exit traffic only, so it is best to avoid these until you need them. Note that you are permitted to turn right on red if it is safe to do so, unless a sign indicates otherwise. STOP for school buses unloading, or you will be fined. Always park the same way round as passing traffic. One thing that may confuse non-US visitors is that overhead street signs indicate *intersections* (the street at right angles, *not* the street you are actually driving on). Speed limits vary from as low as 20mph (32kph) in residential streets to 65mph (104kph) on open freeways. It is generally 55mph (88kph) on highways, and these limits are quite strictly enforced. Sometimes there is a minimum limit, too. Watch out for 'Florida Ice', a mix of water and oil during rain showers that creates extremely slippery driving conditions. Petrol (gas) is still very cheap in the US by European standards, and comes in three grades, all unleaded (about $1.10 a gallon for the cheapest, suitable for a compact car). At gas stations, you have a choice of serve yourself (slightly cheaper), or be served, and perhaps get your windows cleaned at the same time. Some stations have automatic vending machines that accept notes.

Car Rental

Life in the US is highly geared to the motorist, and if you want to do any degree of exploring it is best to have the use of a car. Car hire in Orlando is a good bargain; rates are very competitive, and several tour operators offer such excellent fly-drive deals that it is worth fixing a car up before you arrive. Alamo Rent-a-Car and Dollar are popular agencies used by tour operators, and all the big international firms (Hertz, Avis, Budget) are represented in Orlando. Best rates are weekly, not daily. Make sure you have an unlimited mileage deal, and take out collision damage waiver, along with adequate (that means more than minimal) insurance. Some firms, besides trying to upgrade the car you have booked, will attempt to persuade you to take out massively high insurance cover, which could add as much as 50 per cent to your bill. This is not necessary; nevertheless, bear in mind that many drivers in the US are inadequately insured, and that it is a notoriously litigious society. The reasonably priced 'top-up' cover recommended by some operators is well worth considering for peace of mind. Some car-rental firms impose a surcharge on drivers under 25, and the minimum age is often 21 (sometimes 25 such as with Hertz). Some deals do not allow you to drive outside Florida and Georgia. Visitors from some countries need an International Driver's Permit, and many firms expect you to pay by credit card

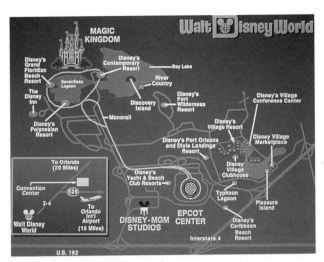

MAGIC KINGDOM

Walt Disney World

Disney's Grand Floridian Beach Resort

Disney's Contemporary Resort

Bay Lake

River Country

Seven Seas Lagoon

The Disney Inn

Discovery Island

Disney's Fort Wilderness Resort

Disney's Village Conference Center

Monorail

Disney's Polynesian Resort

Disney's Village Resort

Disney's Port Orleans and Dixie Landings Resort

Disney Village Marketplace

Disney's Yacht & Beach Club Resorts

Disney Village Clubhouse

To Orlando (20 Miles)

Typhoon Lagoon

Pleasure Island

Convention Center

528

I-4

To Orlando Int'l Airport (15 Miles)

Walt Disney World

DISNEY-MGM STUDIOS

EPCOT CENTER

Disney's Caribbean Beach Resort

Interstate 4

U.S. 192

(see **Money Matters**, page 120). A 'compact' car is the smallest – OK for two, but take something bigger if you have a family and lots of luggage. Nearly all rental cars in the US are automatics, so try to disregard your left leg. They are very easy to get used to, and about as much fun to drive as a milk-float.

Air-conditioning is a standard feature, and one you will be glad of in summer.

The Triple A
The American Automobile Association (AAA) provides certain reciprocal membership facilities to affiliated motoring organisations in other countries, such as the AA. These do not include discounts on accommodation, restaurants or attractions, but their touring guides, routeing and general motoring advice, emergency road rescue – and above all their excellent 'Triptik' strip-

A map will help you plan your time

maps (most other maps of Orlando are abysmal) – are well worth having. The AAA's Orlando office is the national HQ, at Heathrow, heading north of Orlando just off Highway I-4 (Junction 50, Lake Mary Boulevard). Take proof of membership with you, obviously. **American Automobile Association**, 1000 AAA Drive, Heathrow, FL 32746; tel: 444 7188. For emergency roadside assistance, ring 1-800-824 4432 (toll-free).

Electricity
In the US the current is 110–120 volt AC as opposed to the 220-volt current in use in Europe. Plugs have two small flat pins, and foreign appliances without dual voltage will need both a transformer and an adaptor, otherwise an adaptor alone will suffice. If in doubt, ask at your hotel.

Embassies and Consulates

Australia: 636 Fifth Avenue, New York (tel: 212-245 4000).
Canada: 200 South Biscayne Boulevard, Room 160, Miami (tel: 305-579 1600).
Republic of Ireland: 515 Madison Avenue, New York (tel: 212-319 2555).
United Kingdom: Suite 2110, SunBank Tower, 200 South Orange Avenue, Orlando (tel: 407-426 7855).

Emergency Telephone Numbers

Dial 911 for all emergency services, or ask the operator (0) to help you.

Entertainment Information

All over Orlando in hotel

Disney parks have internal transportation

lobbies and other public places you will find racks of free leaflets and visitors' guides galore advertising local attractions. Many holiday hotels have a special guest services desk where you can book any trips or shows. Walt Disney World is splendidly efficient at disseminating information about its own attractions, and understandably more reticent about rival happenings in Orlando (tel: 824 4321). The local newspaper, the *Orlando Sentinel*, gives events listings on Fridays. (See also **Tourist Offices**, page 126.)
Some 'tourist information' booths offering free or discount tickets are actually time-share sellers hoping to persuade you to see (and buy) a property.

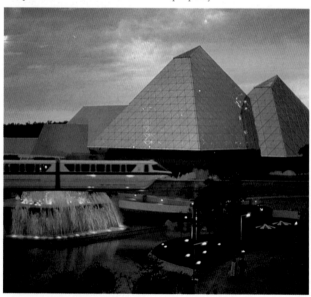

Health

No inoculations are specifically required for Florida, but it is as well to check with your doctor before leaving, and make sure your tetanus jabs are up to date. It is, however, a rabies zone. If you happen to be bitten or scratched by any mammal, wild or domesticated, get medical attention. There have also been several outbreaks of a nasty viral infection called St Louis encephalitis during the last few years. This is carried by mosquitoes. Try to avoid bites by using a good insect repellent containing DEET (diethyltoluamide), and keeping skin covered after dark. By far the most common source of ill health in Florida, however, is too much sun. Wear a hat and sun-screen while you are outside, and make sure that small children take in enough fluid. Minor ailments can be handled by the first aid stations in all the big theme parks. **Center Care**, at 6001 Vineland Road (tel: 351 6682), or the **Buena Vista Walk-in Medical Center**, near WDW Village (tel: 828 3434) are useful. There is a home visit service for hotel guests called **HouseMed** (tel: 648 9234). A convenient hospital in the area is the **Orlando Regional Medical Center**, 1414 South Kuhl Avenue (tel: 841 5111), or the **Sand Lake Hospital**, 9400 Turkey Lake Road (tel: 351 8500). It is very important to make sure that you are adequately insured for any trip to the US, since medical bills can be astronomical, and treatment may simply be withheld if

Don't neglect Orlando's other treats

you have no evidence of the means to pay. A policy offering at least $1,000,000, and preferably unlimited, medical cover is recommended.

Holidays

1 January, New Year's Day; third Monday in January, Martin Luther King's Birthday; third Monday in February, Washington's Birthday; March/April, Good Friday; last Monday in May, Memorial Day; 4 July, Independence Day; first Monday in September, Labor Day; second Monday in October, Columbus Day; 11 November, Veterans' Day; fourth Thursday in November, Thanksgiving Day; 25 December, Christmas Day.

DIRECTORY

Lost Property

The theme parks, especially WDW, are highly organised about lost and found items, including children (name tags; lost children's logbooks). Head for **City Hall** in the Magic Kingdom; **Earth Station** at EPCOT Center, and **Hollywood Boulevard Guest Services** in Disney–MGM Studios. Incidentally, if no one claims an item at WDW, it's finders keepers, so it could be worth being a good citizen and handing something in. Report serious losses to the police or you will not be able to make an insurance claim. Take advantage of the safe deposit boxes at hotels; they are free or very cheap.

Media

Dozens of radio and TV stations bemuse the visitor more or less round the clock. Whatever home comforts your motel does or doesn't have, it will most certainly possess an enormous TV set. Despite the apparent range, there is little enough to choose between most networks; watching or listening in the US is usually an irksome process of channel-zapping through a maze of inferior pop, B-movies and game shows to avoid the commercials. The Public Broadcasting Service shows a more interesting range of programmes and has better news coverage than most. Many motels and hotels feature videos, but you may have to pay extra to hire these, or to watch cable TV. The most widely available local newspaper is the *Orlando*

Sentinel, delivered free to guests in the smarter hotels. You can buy other US national papers in many places, and foreign newspapers too, but the mark-up is high.

Money Matters

It is best to take the bulk of your currency in US dollar traveller's cheques ('checks' in America), including plenty of smallish denominations ($10 or $20). These are widely accepted like ordinary currency in petrol stations, hotels, restaurants, shops, etc, and are, of course, more secure than loose cash. You do not, therefore, need to keep running into banks; in any case, these are not thick on the ground in Orlando, and those that do exist do not generally serve the tourist's *bureau de change* needs. An exception is the **SunBank** (there are several branches in WDW), which can cash and sell traveller's cheques, provide refunds for lost cheques, give cash advances on credit cards, help wire money transfers, etc. You can also exchange foreign currency at lots of places in WDW, including resort hotels, and guest services windows. Beware poor exchange rates in non-Disney hotels. A well-known credit card is one of life's necessities in the US ('Cash or charge?', they'll ask when you pay).

One surprising feature of US currency is that all the notes of whatever denomination are exactly the same size and colour – all greenbacks. So check the numbers. 25¢ (quarters) and 50¢ (half-dollar; rare) coins

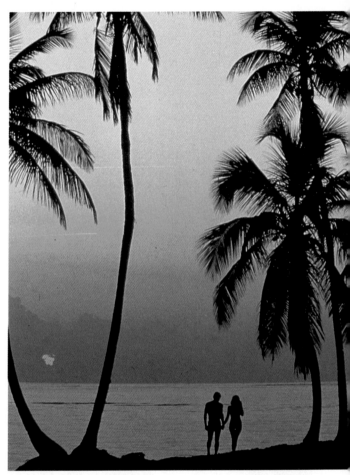

are useful for telephone calls, toll roads, buses, stamp machines (but see **Post Office**, page 123). Single dollar bills are handy for tips (an all-pervasive US custom). The 6 per cent sales tax added to practically everything in Florida results in curiously irregular final bills, which means your

Choose your own theme holiday

pocket or purse rapidly silts up with pennies (1¢), nickels (5¢) and dimes (10¢). At some point you will have to think of a way of disposing of these. Visitors to Walt Disney World will encounter another sign of the Mouse's might: Mickey

even has his own currency.
Disney Dollars are fun for kids.
They can be obtained from
ticket booths, guest relations
and resort hotels, and can be
used to purchase food or
souvenirs anywhere within
WDW. There is no mark-up on
them, and they are redeemable
for greenbacks at any time.

Opening Times
SunBanks are generally open
from 09.00 to 16.00hrs Monday
to Friday (closed at weekends).
The branch at Orlando
International Airport is open
Monday–Friday 08.00–
18.00hrs, Saturday 08.00–
17.00hrs. Many shops do not
open before 10.00hrs, but do
not shut till 18.00hrs or so,
Monday to Saturday. Most malls
and shopping centres,
however, are open Monday–
Saturday 10.00–21.00hrs,
Sunday 12.00–18.00hrs. Theme
park shops follow the park
opening hours.
Major theme park opening
times vary greatly, depending
on seasonal demand, and may
change at short notice. In high
season they open early
(generally from 08.30hrs), and
stay open late, sometimes till
midnight. But check carefully
during your stay, or you could
be caught out. (See also page
20.) Some museums close on
Mondays. Post Offices usually
open Monday–Friday 09.00–
17.00hrs,but many hotels and
major attractions provide a post
office service for longer hours.

Personal Safety
Orlando is not generally a
dangerous place. So far, the
major theme parks have kept
an admirable safety record,
particularly Walt Disney World.
But accidents are not unknown.
Particular attention should be
paid to all warning notices and
announcements (keeping your
hands and arms clear of moving
equipment, not jumping from
car to car, etc). These are, after
all, thrill rides, and as such
entail certain hazards. Do not
do the scary things (such as

Sorcery in the Sky

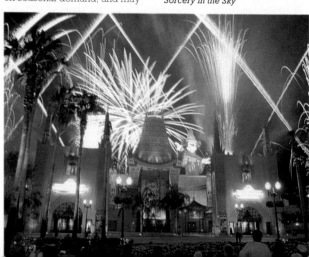

Space Mountain) if you are pregnant, or if you have a bad back or neck – if in doubt, check with your doctor before leaving. G-force stresses are very noticeable on some rides. Motion sickness and dizziness are obvious contra-indications, though few rides last long enough to cause many problems.

Alligators are found in fresh water everywhere in the state, and are extremely dangerous – do not feed or molest them in any way. Although rarely aggressive unless they are bothered, they can come out of the water and outrun a horse over a short distance. Never allow small children or pets to approach an alligator *under any circumstances*, and do not swim if alligators are present. If you are bitten, even by a very small alligator, seek medical attention immediately.

Pharmacies

You can buy simple medicaments at any drug store, though certain drugs generally available elsewhere require a prescription in the US. Acetaminophen is the US equivalent of paracetamol. A couple of downtown pharmacies (**Ekerd Drugs**, 908 Lee Road; **Walgreen Drug Store**, International Drive) stay open all night. Holiday hotels, particularly in WDW, can always help out with a plaster or aspirin.

Places of Worship

WDW caters for multifarious creeds. Protestants can head for Luau Cove at the Polynesian Village (Sundays at 09.00hrs);

Catholics get in earlier (at 08.00hrs), or later (at 10.15hrs). Check with guest services. There are plenty of churches (Baptist, Presbyterian, Methodist, you name it) all over Orlando, and a couple of synagogues too (liberal and conservative). If you are into spiritualism, head for Cassadaga (see page 79). The *Orlando Sentinel* gives details of church services on Saturdays.

Police

Dial **911** if you want them. If you don't, stick to the speed limits and don't drink and drive – the penalties for drink-driving offences are severe. In this tourist-oriented region, however, the police are friendly and courteous towards foreigners, and fairly tolerant of minor misdemeanours or confusions.

City police deal with local crime; the Highway Patrol deal with traffic violations and look out for motorists stranded by the roadside. Pull over, raise the bonnet lid and put your hazard lights on if you are in trouble.

Post Office

They do exist (there is a useful one at the Lake Buena Vista Crossroads shopping center in WDW), but are thin on the ground; a request for stamps is generally met by a wave towards a vending machine. Besides requiring vast amounts of small change, these charge a 25 per cent premium. It is best to buy them at the reception of any WDW resort hotel, or the information offices (e.g., **City Hall** in The Magic Kingdom) of the big parks (see also **Opening Times**, page 122).

Public Transport

Air

Orlando is now a major routeing hub. You can fly non-stop to Orlando from about 50 different US cities, on over a dozen airlines (see also **Arriving**, page 113).

Bus

Greyhound Lines serve Orlando from many centres in the US; within the metropolitan Orlando area, local buses provide a good service, notably the **Gray Line**, which serves the airport and most of Orlando's main attractions and hotels (tel: 422 0744). Many hotels have their own courtesy buses, and WDW has an entire fleet of efficient, clearly flagged buses whirling constantly around, all completely free for resort guests (see page 21).

Rail

AmTrak serves Orlando, also stopping at Winter Park and Sanford north of the city, and Kissimmee near WDW (for general information, tel: 1-800 872 7245, toll-free).

Taxi

These are too expensive ($2.25 for the first mile, $1.30 for each additional mile) to be a sensible option for anything other than occasional or short-distance hops, but if money really is no object, limousine transport can easily be arranged through your hotel's guest services desk.

Senior Citizens (Seniors)

Florida attracts huge numbers of elderly visitors and permanent residents, many of whom feel young enough at heart for a trip to Walt Disney World. Saga International Holidays, a specialist operator for the elderly, has a package programme to Orlando. AARPs (American Association of Retired Persons, over 50) are eligible (with ID) for discounts on accommodation, meals, car rental, transport, and many of the attraction charges in the Orlando area; other discounts are available for the over 60s. Staff at WDW and other theme parks should be able to help with any special needs.

Student and Youth Travel

While it is true that most concessions at the major theme parks apply to children (under 17), some attractions and sights offer special admission prices for bona fide students, and there are also concessionary rail fares (International Student Identity Card as proof).

Telephones

Available in lots of public places (hotel lobbies, drug stores, restaurants, garages and at the roadside). You need 5¢, 10¢ or 25¢ coins (local calls usually cost 25¢, but local calls from some of the small private telephone companies' phones may cost $2 or more). For **assistance** dial the operator (0). For local directory enquiries, dial 411. 'Collect' means reverse the charges. Orlando spans several telephone areas, and calling Walt Disney World from downtown is long-distance. The area code for Orlando is 407.

For **long-distance** within the area code, dial 1 plus the number. Outside the area code, dial 1, plus code, plus number. Note that long-distance calls from hotel rooms attract a high mark-up.
Cheap rates apply after 17.00hrs, even cheaper between 23.00 and 08.00hrs. Many hotels, airlines, attractions, etc, have toll-free (free of charge) numbers for potential customers – look out for numbers beginning with 800.

To call abroad from the USA, dial 011 plus the country code (44 UK; 353 Eire; 1 Canada; 61 Australia; 64 New Zealand), the area code minus the initial '0', then the number. For the USA from Britain dial 010 1 (00 1 from April 95) and the area code (407 Orlando) and the number.

Main Street, USA and Cinderella Castle in Walt Disney World

Time

Local time is Eastern Standard (same as New York), which is five hours behind GMT. Daylight saving applies, with clocks an hour ahead between April and October. A note on dates: the US convention is month/day/year (thus 13 December 1991 = 12.13.91).

Tipping

Definitely a feature of the democratic egalitarian society. Customers are forcefully reminded that *Gratuities Are Not Included* as they stump up for a meal, though in some places a service charge is automatically added. Staff rely heavily on tips to make a decent living. At Walt Disney World, however, staff do not hover for tips, and indeed are not permitted to accept them in the fast-food restaurants, but as elsewhere it is customary in restaurants with table service (between 10 and 20 per cent). However, attractions that feature dinner usually include gratuities, and no extra is required. Cabbies expect around 15 per cent; porters 50¢ a bag (a dollar is the minimum you can decently proffer).

Toilets

Known euphemistically as 'rest rooms' in the US, also as 'the men's/ladies' room', more excruciatingly as 'comfort stations'. In a private house, you would ask for the 'bathroom'. They are nearly always well kept, and free.

Tourist Offices

The Orlando/Orange County Convention and Visitors' Bureau has an **information centre** in the Mercado Mediterranean Shopping Village at 8445 International Drive (tel: 363 5871; open: daily 08.00 to 20.00hrs) and at 8723 International Drive, where you can pick up stacks of leaflets and brochures about what's on, including the free *Visitor's Guide*, plus discount coupons. There is another centre at **Kissimmee**, 2.5 miles (4km) east of I-4 on US192, at 1925 East Irlo Bronson Memorial Highway, PO Box 42 2007, Kissimmee, FL 34742-2007 (tel: 847 5000).

Disney operates its own vastly efficient network of information centres all over the world: in Britain (written enquiries only) contact **Walt Disney Attractions**, Beaumont House, Kensington Village, Avonmore Road, London W14 8TS (supply a useful information consume pack – written enquiries only). For pre-trip information from the UK, contact the **Orlando Tourism Bureau**, 18–24 Westbourne Grove, London W2 5RH (tel: 020 7243 8072), the **US Travel and Tourism Administration**, PO Box 1EN, London W1A 1EN (tel: 020 7439 7433), or the **Visit Florida** office, Roebuck House, Palace Street, London SW1E 5BA (tel: 0891 600 555).

Travel Agencies

Almost any large holiday hotel will have a guest services desk with information on car hire, local attractions, reservations, etc. Offices advertising tours and tickets can be found in all the main visitor areas.